BELIEVE IN YOURSELF

MANIFEST THE BEST YOU

CHANELL FAIR

Copyright © 2019 Chanell Fairclough

All rights reserved. No part of this publication may be reproduced, distributed, or transmitted in any form or by any means, including photocopying, recording, or other electronic or mechanical methods, without the prior written permission of the publisher, except in the case of brief quotations embodied in reviews and certain other non-commercial uses permitted by copyright law.

Any internet addresses, phone numbers, or company or product information printed in this book are offered as a resource and are not intended in any way to be or to imply an endorsement by the publisher, nor does the publisher vouch for the existence, content, or services of these sites, phone numbers, companies, or products beyond the life of this book

ISBN 978-1-7342191-0-4

ISBN: 1-7342191-1-1

Published by Believe In Your Book Publishing

Printed in the United States of America

For permission request, write to the publisher, addressed "Attention: Permissions Coordinator/ to the address below.

Email: chanellfair@gmail.com

Hey Love,

Congrats, on starting your journey in Believing In Yourself! You are wonderfully, uniquely made and you have something incredible to offer the world. Be true to who you are and let's proceed to becoming the BEST version of you. I believe you can and I know you will!

As you are flipping through these pages, you will find spiritual inspiration that will help you gain insight on facilitating emotional healing and assistance with moving past frustrating habits and disappointments. Ultimately, you will learn how to live the best life by prioritizing, being consistent and using my long life strategies to achieve success..

My goal in writing this book is to guide you in releasing all of the negative thoughts, hurt and insecurities that are holding you back from your destination. I want to show you how to replace it with clarity, operate in your purpose and give you the tools you need to achieve everything your heart desires.

You will be educated, coached to exude confidence, developed a belief system and also inspired to follow your dreams and goals to become successful.

Again, congrats on starting your journey to a better you. Not only is it important for others to believe in you, but it is most important for you to believe in yourself!

I BELIEVE IN YOU!

Love,
Chanell Fair

CONTENTS

Foreword……………………………………..…………..i
Dedication………………………………………………..ii
Introduction……..………………………………..………iii
Chapter 1- Revealing Your Truth…………………….1
Chapter 2- Be You, Be Confident………………….15
Chapter 3- Manifest Your Dreams……………….29
Chapter 4- Your Circle………………………………..…43
Chapter 5- Renew Your Mind…………..…………..51
Chapter 6- Silence……………………………..………..67
Chapter 7- Clarity………………………..…..……….77
Chapter 8- Vision …………….……………………..91
Chapter 9- Keep Winning...101
My Journey to Believing in Myself………………109
I AM………………………………………………………..115

FOREWORD

As a Commissioner in the City of Miramar, I would like to thank you for purchasing this life-changing book by our very own **Chanell Fair,** a graduate of Miramar High School. I am very proud of her and wish her continued success as she follows her dreams to become a legendary writer and inspiring motivator.

There are times in everyone's life when we experience difficult and hard times. It is during those times that we must challenge ourselves to do something different or unexpected to move us out of the darkness. But what should we do? This book offers inspirational stories and anecdotes as well as specific tasks for the reader to accomplish. As each task is accomplished, a new perspective is gained.

When I was a child, I never thought of running for office, but the older I got, I knew I wanted to make a difference in my community. I wanted to impact lives and be part of a community that my family, and I were proud to call home. My journey was not always easy, but I never gave up. There were times I doubted myself and my skills, but I surrounded myself with positive people and continued to learn and grow. I encourage each of you to believe in yourself and break through anything that is holding you back from following your passion in life.

After reading **Believe in Yourself, Manifest the Best You**, I am confident you will have the tools to accomplish your dreams. As you complete the steps outlined in the book, you will change your attitude as you move towards your goals. It took time, patience and perseverance to get where I am. Today, as a Commissioner in the beautiful City of Miramar, I am doing what I love every day. I wish the same for you, so pursue your dreams with love and passion!

Commissioner Maxwell B. Chambers,
City of Miramar, Florida

DEDICATION

First, to my Lord and Savior **Jesus Christ**, the centerpiece of my life, the creator of my conviction and the yoke that keeps my family together, Thank You LORD! To my amazing husband **Michael**, who has always believed > and motivated me through tough times because Lord knows that I have had some rough days. I just want to say **Thank You! Thank You,** for everything you have done for me and our **beautiful children,** especially being patient with us, while the best was in process. *I Love You!*

To my four wonderful, unique and creative children, **Sanaii, Makaii, Delano** and **Leilani** mommy *loves* you and *thank you* for teaching me about unconditional love. You are my greatest blessing *God* has giving me, and I love you with all of my heart!

To my **Mother Stacy and Father Anthony**, words cannot express the joy I have in my heart to see the look on your faces of being proud of your youngest daughter, ME! Thank you for loving me! To my stepmother, **Nicole**, who has also treated me as her own and loved me, Thank You!

To my amazing sisters **Shaina, Chana, Keron, Toni-Ann, Shanice** and brothers **Nyann, Ramesh, Rasheed, Troy & Damany,** who have shared many joyful moments and will continue to have incredible laughter and happiness. I love you and thank you for being there for me! To my **In-Laws, Sandy, Keisha, Twan,** and **Mike (RIP)** thank you for welcoming me into your family!

To my amazing best friend **Yaninna,** who never judge me but always loved me like a sister. I want to say thank you so much for being that shoulder to cry on and that inspiration to move and drive me to the next level in life. In addition, to my good friends **Erika, Tonya, Jasmyn & Audrey** thank you for motivating me! To all of my colleagues, former co-workers and extended family, a Huge Thank You!

To my **Pastor's, Dennis & Zellia Smith,** thank you for believing in me and helping on my spiritual journey. "Your prayers will not go in vain."

Lastly, to all of my clients, thank you for believing in the process and in me. I pray you continue to inspire me to inspire you to greatness. Thank you!

INTRODUCTION

Welcome, Welcome!

Thank You in advance for purchasing my book and I pray that it will enhance your inner spirit as well as your ambitions in life. Just a brief synopsis of what to expect. However, before we get started, please strap your seatbelt on, have an open mind and get ready for a change. This book touches on every aspect of life's ups and downs and this will be a ride of your life. The book will show you how to release all of the negative thoughts, hurt, depression and insecurities that will allow you to take back your stability and sanity. Also, how to gain clarity, operate in your purpose and the tools you need to achieve everything your heart desire.

In this walk of life, I have observed many individuals that are broken, hurt, depressed and lack confidence, which leaves them vulnerable and having distorted thinking along with feeling insecure. They feel stuck, unaccomplished, defeated and feel as if they have no way out their debacle. We all have dreams, goals, and ambition that we want to accomplish, but often too many times we sabotage ourselves out of our ambition or we do not believe enough in our dreams to pursue it.

As a wife, mother of four children, Life Coach, Educator and Mentor, I also understand how it feels to not put forth my best effort, such as being broken blaming life, unappreciated and insecure. I, too, have gone through, dealt with, a multitude of pain, hurt, abandonment, and felt like I would never live the life I desired to live. After being a teen mom twice, I was hurt, insecure, spiritually immature, and not feeling good enough. I applied these principles to rebuild my spirit and my strength. Today, I live the *BEST* life that God has given me because he had a plan for me." For I know the plans I have for you,' declares the Lord, plans" to prosper you and not harm you, plans to give you hope and a future. (*Jeremiah 29:11*)

By reading this book, you will live a life of clarity, regain your self-worth, believe in yourself, operate in your purpose and receive nuggets to catapult you into greatness as you plan for success. No longer living to please others, but only to please God and yourself.

Your time is now! If you are ready to live life to the fullest. No more worry, hurt, shame, feeling unappreciated and no more putting yourself off. It is time to invest in self-development, self-confidence, and self-worth.

This book will help you flourish in both your personal life and relationships. You will be able to manifest every dream and goal you once had.

After reading this book, you will be **CONFIDENT, FEARLESS** and **UNAPOLOGETIC.** No more living below your means and your value. **THE TIME IS NOW!**

Chapter 1
~REVEALING YOUR TRUTH~

WHY ARE PEOPLE DEPRESSED?

"Change your thoughts and change your situation "~Anonymous

Many people are depressed and unhappy with their situations, such as their jobs, where they live and most importantly, the amount of money they make. Unfortunately, in this world that we live in, money dictates who you are and your status. The more money you make, the better chance of a person you are. In addition, people tend to think this is true, to live comfortably in a world of traditions. This mindset is a false sense of reality and most of all, it's not true. You see, we live in a very superficial world, which causes people to live a superficial life and not be true to who they are. Many people do not know who they are and their true value. When people live below their means, it causes them to be unhappy and depressed.

Does that sound familiar? Are you living the best life you can? Alternatively, are you living below your standards? When God created you, there is something that you single-handedly have to accomplish for you to fulfill your purpose. You may know exactly what it is or you may not quite understand what it is yet.

Living a mediocre life is not what God wants you to do. He said: "He came so we can have a life exceeding, abundantly, above all which we can ask (***John 10:10***)." So, if your Heavenly Father stated that in scripture then, why are you living below your standards?

You have something great inside of you, and it is important that you live the life God intended for you to live.

Unfortunately, many people are not motivated and continue living below their desired standards. Not only does living below your standards affect you, but it also affects people around you.

There is a saying, "your destiny is wrapped up in others." In this life, it is not just about you, and it's about how you make others around you better. What you do every day affects you and the people around you.

Any form of stress, depression or hurt is a tool the enemy uses to keep you down and to make you feel like you are not worth anything. It's hard to see the good side of a situation when all you feel is depressed, stressed and hurt.

People Hurt

When people are hurting, they tend to treat others the way they are feeling. When you are going through situations whether if it's good or bad, it affects those around you.

A manager of a company lived a super stressed out life. Daily she would come to work with such a nasty attitude. All the employees would talk about her ugly attitude. Little did they know, a couple of years back the manager possess good spirit until she went to the doctor and received some heart failing news. The doctor revealed to her that she was diagnosed with a tumor in her brain. The information shifted her entire outlook on life. After the manager received the news, she began to live life the best way she knew how. In this case, some people allow bad situations make them better, and other people let the unfortunate circumstances dictate their outcome. She was one! She no longer cared about others feelings. Therefore, the manager was hurting and had no problem with treating others in the same negative manner.

The employees avoided her as much as possible in fear that they would be either ridiculed or written up. She had such a negative outlook on every situation that came up. The employees did not understand why she behaved in that manner until the information was exposed. Quickly the employees' shifted how they felt and started to feel sorry for their manager.

Just because an individual is hurting does not give them the right to treat others poorly. However, many people that are hurting have a pattern of doing just that.

Obstacle to Opportunity

"It is better to be prepared for an opportunity and not have one than to have an opportunity and not be prepared." - Whitney Young

We all like to think life is just this fantastic walk. That nothing terrible will ever happen to us. In addition, we believe life is all peace, love, and happiness. I am not saying this cannot be true, but what I will say is before the peace, love and happiness stage you will have some monkey wrenches and hiccups along the way.

Sometimes in life we all get a hand dealt that we had no control over. We had no control over the parents we have, the family we were raised in, or the type of surrounding we grow up with. Regardless of the hand that you were dealt, the goal is to make the best of it. No matter the obstacles or situations that may occur.

Some obstacles may be big and some may be small, but no matter the size, it is a setup for an opportunity. Be prepared for an opportunity!

Do not let the hand that you were dealt, cause you not to win the game of life. Many times, in card games the person with the worst hand comes back and wins the whole game. This can be you! It will take hard work, focus, and determination, but it can be done.

One time, I met a young lady, and she had such a beautiful personality, spirit and heart. Nevertheless, I overheard people talking about her, and they judged her based on how she looked. She came from an impoverished and tough neighborhood. It is unfortunate that people will judge others without getting to know that person. The young lady knew that people judged her, but she did not allow that to stop her from being a sweet and positive person. She was determined to be someone great in life despite what others thought of her.

Don't let your past dictate where you are going in life. You have the opportunity to be, live and become the best person you desire to be.

Situations will arise and when sought through, a chance for an opportunity will show up. Do not be discouraged because of the roadblocks, or detours. It is just a setback for a setup.

When that opportunity presents itself, you need to be ready!

F.E.A.R

False Evidence Appearing Real,
Or
Face Everything And Rise

Do not allow fear to hold you back from being the best you. Whatever desires you have, you can achieve them. Do not let FEAR stop you from being great.

Life is too short to allow fear to cripple you and keep you from moving forward. Many people turn to drugs, alcohol or smoking to help ease the pain of fear and anxiety.

Don't be afraid of life. When you think about your situation, you start to realize that someone is in the worst situation than you. Most of the times, the things that you fear is not life threatening. What is the worst that can happen?

When life can no longer threaten you with death, what else is there?

Starting that business, writing that book or speaking in front of a large crowd will not kill you. You have to step out on **Faith** and face everything and rise.

(Job 4:10)
The lion may roar and growl, yet the teeth of the great lions are broken.

Too many times, I found myself in this situation. Filled with so much fear. Afraid of what people would think about me, so I lived my life in complete fear. Every time I wanted to do something, I would stop and think about what others would say, and would just talk myself out of it. To be honest, I was braver when I was a child. I was super daring, ambitious and did not care what others thought. Then, I became an adult. After becoming an adult, all of my ambition, bravery, and boldness went out the window.

All of my fears just overwhelmed me, and I was afraid to do this, I was scared to do that. I started to think to myself, "what is wrong with me?" I had to change my mindset to positive mode! "This have to come to an end," and it did.

Fear can either motivate you or cripple you. Celebrities like Jay-Z, Beyoncé and many more still have anxiety issue before going out on stage in front of millions of people. You would never know because even though they are afraid, they rise and go out on stage and give it all they got. They allowed **fear to motivate them.**

Fear can also be used as a blocker or building blocks.

Fear of being diagnosed with a health scare will motivate people to lose weight. They will no longer say they are big boned. I have never seen a fat skeleton… lol, have you? Others will feel sorry for themselves and hope other people will feel empathy towards them.

Have you ever heard of people fearing success or being Wealthy? It sounds crazy, but many people suffer from the overwhelming feeling of success.

Think about babies taking their first steps. In the beginning, they may be a little afraid, but they keep trying. No matter how many times they fall or get hurt, they keep working until they get it right. Babies do not allow anything or anyone to stop them from taking their first steps. They get back up and keep trying until they succeed.

Fear can motivate you... Diagnosis will make people get their health in order; such as lose weight/ big boned or not. Remember that fat skeleton. LOL

Yes, life happens, obstacles may come, things may not go the way you planned; however, you have to continue to push through to get what you want out of life.

Do Not Let Regret & Fear Replace Your Dreams

I should have,
I could have,
I would have,
However, I did not.

In actuality, if you want to do something ***JUST DO IT***! In addition, I know, it is easier said than done, but it is just that simple.

Regret will only bring you down and make you feel like you are a failure.

People are always quick to tell you, what you are not doing and what you need to do. Instead of telling you, what they like about what you did. It is your job to encourage yourself and be content with the decisions that you make.

If you do not like the decisions that you have made, change them. Start owning your decisions and making sure that you are happy with the future choices that you make. It is your life, and it is time to take ownership of it.

Your dreams and goals are super important to you. Do not let false evidence appearing real; stop you from accomplishing your dreams and goals.

You can achieve your goals and dream. Here is a scripture:

(Philippians 4:13)
I can do all things through Christ who gives me strength.

The Lord is with you at all times. Even when you feel weak, He is there. He will give you what you need to get you to where you need to go. God knows the desire of your heart; He wants you to give it to Him. Every hurt, pain or weakness, God is waiting with open arms to help you. You can do it.

If you want to start that business, do it! If you are going to write that book, do it! If you are going to go for that promotion on the job, go for it! Face Everything and Rise. You can do it!

What would your life look like if you did not allow your fear to creep in and stop you?

Take a moment, close your eyes and meditate… What does it look and feel like if you accomplished your goals and eliminated FEAR?

Stop Procrastinating

A study shows that 20% of people consider themselves as chronic procrastinators. Procrastination is the lack of self-motivation. It is the fast route to killing your dreams and goals.

A man named Bill decided that he was going to stop allowing procrastinating to defeat him and decided to buy a book called 50 Steps to Defeating Procrastination. It has been a little over ten years, and he still is trying to schedule a time to read the book.

Do not be like Bill. When you put your mind to something, get it done. Procrastination is the thief of time.

Back in college, I can remember my professor giving the class a paper due the following week. Being the kind of college student I was, I would wait until the night before and pull an all-nighter because of direct procrastination.

Unfortunately, this behavior has spilled over into real life and procrastination have become the killer for many people dreams and goals.

Time is valuable, important and you can never get it back. Prioritize your goals and get them done.

Waiting until the time is right or when you get that time from your busy schedule to do something may take forever to get there.
You will be waiting all of your life to complete something that can change your life: if you will only stop procrastinating.

Stop letting Social Media control your day. Social Media is another form of procrastination. So many people spend numerous hours on social media. Such as spending 2 hours a day, 14 hours a week and averaging about 56 hours a month just scrolling and watching others live a fake life is not productive. If you spent 56 hours a month focusing on your dreams and goals, you would be successful in achieving your dreams?

Another essential tool to stop procrastination is writing a daily to-do list. This can help you prioritize your day. However, if you are writing the same to do list every day and not completing the task at hand, you will be procrastinating. When you make your daily to-do list be sure to achieve as much as possible, starting with the most important task moving to the less important task. Do not leave the hard task for last. Do it first, then everything after that will be a breeze.

If you continue to put your to-do list off, it will continue to grow and will make you feel overwhelmed and unaccomplished. You have the willpower to complete whatever it is that you put your mind to.

Stop Being Basic

If God created you in His image, why are you living below your value?

I am not just talking about spending money on yourselves to feel good. I am talking about living like royalty, feeling like royalty and acting like royalty.

If you are a Child of the Most High, you have inherited what your heavenly **Father** has. You should live and treat yourself as such.

Also, if you lived how God sees you, it will eliminate stress and depression. You have to believe that you are amazing and worth living an amazing and incredible life. Being basic should not be in your vocabulary. You are royalty and if you believe that, now is the time to start speaking, acting and living like royalty.

If you were a King or a Queen, would you act the way you're currently acting now?

Would you dress the way you're currently dressing?
Would you entertain the people that are currently in your life?
Would you put up with the things you currently putting up with?

For instance, I asked my son, "Why were you misbehaving in school today?" he said, "I don't know! Mommy" and in return, I said, "What if we as a family found out that Mommy was a daughter of the Emperor of a country?"

"How would you feel?" He said, "Oh Mommy, I will be super excited!"

I said, "will you tell anyone?" and he said, "Yes, mommy I will tell everyone!" Then I asked him, "How would you act?"

Then he said, " I will walk around with my head up high, and when I get to class, I will sit down in my chair slow so everyone can see me," I laughed and said, "Okay, how will you acted inside of the class?"

He said," I will act like the boss." I said and "how does a boss act?" He said, very stern and focused".

I responded exactly! So just to let you know mommy is a daughter of a King, which means you are a grandson of a king, He says, "huh" Is grandpa a King? I said, No, Jesus Christ is the King of all Kings, so this point forward I need you to act like royalty that you are"!

A quick lesson learned that you need to stop being basic or not valuing yourselves and take more pride in who you are and whose you are.

Only the Strong Will Survive- Stop Being Weak

Being weak and trying to survive in this life will not work. In this life, we all have heard that this life will chew you up and spit you out.
Just like the story of David and Goliath. Even though Goliath was strong and supposedly David was weak, it was David who had the spirit of God on his side.

Actuality David was strong spiritually. So let me explain, when I say the strong will survive I'm talking about strong spiritually and not physically. All of our battles are physical which stems from the spiritual world. Learning how to strengthen your spiritual life through reading God's word and prayer will help you conquer many battles.

Stop Comparing Yourself

Comparing yourself to others deprives you of your joy, happiness, value, and meaning. The joy in your life keeps you going but comparing yourself to others is stealing your joy.

Comparing yourselves to others, you gain nothing at all, but you lose everything.

Comparing yourself is unfair. You always want to compare yourself to people who are super successful and seem to have it all together. Let's not even mention those on Social Media we all know everyone always put forth their best foot meaning they only show the good side of their situation when in actuality there is more to their story.

Time is valuable and comparing yourselves to others, you are robbing yourselves of precious time when you could be using that time wisely.

You could take that time and focus on getting yourselves on point meaning getting yourselves together. You can make that time for self-development or spending time with God. Instead of focusing on other people's happiness instead of creating your own happiness.

God has created every one of us uniquely, wonderfully and fearfully. It is our job to live out this amazing life that God has created for us. We have to remember when God created us he said we were "Good."

(Psalms 139:14)
I praise you because I am fearfully and wonderfully made: your works are wonderful

There could only be one of me, and my job is to be the best version I can be and not to try to be anyone else.

Today it is your turn to live this amazing life of being the best version of YOU.

Stop comparing yourself and start being and living the best life you can as the best version of you!

All Lights Green

Waiting for all the lights to be green to be a better version of you, you will be waiting a lifetime for that perfect moment.

Was there ever a time you sat at home with your car keys in your hand, saying you cannot leave the house because you are waiting for all the streetlights to turn green. In reality, you leave your home and head to your destination without a second thought in mind of what color the streetlights are.

Waiting until the time is right will never get you to where you want to go.

Heading out of your house with your keys in hand, you can get to your destination even if you encounter a couple of red lights here or there. It may delay your time of getting to your destination, but it will not take you off your course if you stay focus on what is ahead.

It will never be the right time for you to get up and go after what it is that you want to do.

It is easy to come up with a reason why you should wait such as, you not having enough money, time or resources. Then, when you do get the money, the time and the resources another excuse will populate as to why you cannot move forward.

What if God said, He would not bless you until you were perfect. Until you have it all together. You will be in a bitter place with God because we are not perfect and will never be perfect.

If your Heavenly Father is willing to work with you just how you are, you should be willing to move forward in his glory. Not waiting until the time is right or until all the lights are green. He has guided your footsteps to success, all you have to do is stay the course and trust Him.

Obstacles will always come up and try to stop you, but you have to trust yourself and understand that greater waits for you. Thanks to God, He does not operate how we do. We are so easy to give up and let go. We are saved by grace.

Let it Go!

Letting go and stop having excuses for every little activity that hinders you from being great.

It is time out for you to let go of every situation that have hurt you.

God has created you for a reason, with a purpose, and on purpose. There is a job that God created that only **you** can fulfill. That job will not be complete unless you complete it. No one else can get the job done but you.

Therefore, whatever it is that is stopping you from fulfilling your true purpose, let it go!

For instance, it can be a man, a woman, a habit, excuses, hurt, shame, procrastination, or anything that you can think of that is holding you back from being the Best version of you. It is time to let it go!

Let nothing stop you from being whom God created you to be and fulfilling the promises and the purpose God has put in your life.

Let Go and Let God! God will direct your path, and at any time you feel like you cannot do it, call on Him and He will come.

God is waiting for you to call on Him and cast all of your burdens on Him.

(Psalms 55:22)
Cast your cares on the Lord, and He will sustain you: He will never let the righteous be shaken.

The battle, the stress and the hurt is too much for you to bare this is why the bible says the battle is not yours it belongs to the Lord. The Lord knew that at times situations were going to be tough. That does not mean that you are not going to go through anything.

You are human, and you are going to encounter hurt, mistreatment and feel unhappy; however, the goal is not to stay there.

You have to go through and be sure not to stay there. You have too much to offer this world; too many people depend on you. It is your responsibility to get up each day and start with a renewed mind. You have to focus on the prize and know that God is there with you and you are not alone.

He loves you so much, and He wants you to live the best life that He have created for you. Therefore, from this point forward, whatever is putting you in a box let it go and give it to God and keep moving forward.

BELIEVE IN YOURSELF · 14

CHAPTER 2
~*BE YOU, BE CONFIDENT*~

WHAT IS CONFIDENCE?

Confidence is the feeling or belief that one can rely on someone or something; firm trust. Which means this feeling is something that can be taught. If someone lacks confidence in a particular area of their life and then learn the importance of faith; then they can become confident.

Some people believe that certain individuals were born with this super confidence and that is not true. Their story usually start by saying, "they once were very shy or timid, and then they found this inner power and Boom! They became tremendous and super confident.

Being upset, angry, excited, happy & sad are all actual feelings. In seconds, if you were sad and someone said something funny, you can instantly change how you feel and start laughing. Same with being excited. You can be super excited, someone can say something that you do not agree with, and just like that, you'll get upset.

A little girl thought to herself that she was never enough and was never good enough in all areas. She looked to her parents to help with building her self-esteem, but they were too busy working on themselves. She felt she was not getting the attention that she wanted, so she turned to boys. She met a boy, and he told her all the things she wanted to hear. After hearing all those great things, he took advantage of her. She got the attention that she thought she wanted but it only lasted for a moment. After the boy got what he wanted, he no longer gave her the attention that she craved.

She decided in her later years to no longer seek attention from others and started looking within. She develops a relationship with Christ, she began to work on inner spirit, and her confidence started to go through the roof. She understood who she was and whom she belongs to.

Everything you need you already have. You do not need anyone to tell you that you are great and you can do it. You need to believe in yourself and encourage yourself. Others may say to you how great you are, but when you get to a place that you know how great you are because you were created in God's image. No one can take that away from you.

Self Confidence is a feeling of trust in one's abilities, qualities, and judgment. Building self-confidence and self-esteem look at the keywords. SELF.... It's about you. Not waiting for others to build your self-esteem. If you wait for others to build your self-esteem you will be waiting for a lifetime. Continually building your own confidence is essential.

Focus On You

It's okay to be selfish. **Selfish** meaning take time to focus on your**self**. You may find yourself focusing on pleasing others. For example, mothers are number one with losing themselves, to helping others. They put so much energy into their family and leave themselves for last. I am not saying that you are supposed to leave your children and husband for last. What I am saying is that it is okay to take care of yourself. When you are happy, it is easier to care of others.

Happy wife, happy life. When you are happy, it is easy to lend a helping hand to others in need. However, when you are unhappy, it is not a pleasant feeling doing for others. You start to feel irritated, frustrated and upset. Therefore, focus on making you happy and it will be easier to help those around you.

Think about what makes you unhappy, and then think about ways you can make that situation better. What are positive activities that you can do to make you feel great again?

Give Compliments!

Giving in every aspect is super important. The bible says we must give.

(2 Corinthians 9:7)

Every man according as he purposeth in his heart, so let him give; not grudgingly, nor of necessity, for GOD LOVETH A CHEERFUL GIVER.

In all things we must give:

Can we give with words? Can we give compliments? Can we give with time? Can we give with things, other than **money**?

When people hear the word "give" they think of money. We can give with so much more.

So many times people will see others and like what they are wearing or what they are saying, but will never acknowledge them.

Certain women we will see a young lady looking remarkable from head to toe and will not even say, Hi! You look nice today.... It seems to be hard for some woman to compliment another woman, but they in return always want someone to compliment them.

You may think that this is not important or not that serious, whoever, it is. We need to learn how to give in all areas of life; not just tithes or helping someone around us.

We need to also give with words and encouragement.

You can change someone's entire day just by telling him or her something good about himself or herself. On the other hand, people love to receive compliments with no problem, but for some people it is hard to give.

Just try it, I promise when you see the impact you have on someone just by telling them.

Here are a couple of saying to enhance compliments:

> You look nice today
>
> I like your hair
>
> I really like your tie
>
> That shirt fits you well and the big one…
>
> Are you working out? You look good.

Everyone loves to hear that one, lol!

Give a compliment without looking for something in return. It will make your day go by a lot better. Start identifying the good in others and others will do the same with you.

It starts with you.

Do not wait for someone to compliment you; you do it first. Get in the habit of praising others first.

Be a cheerful compliment giver. Watch and see the feeling you will have and the reaction of the person you are complimenting.

Get in the habit of doing it frequently. Let complimenting people be a part of who you are. See the good in others.

It takes 21 days to start a new habit not one day. So be fearless, try complimenting others for the next 21 days, and see the difference.

Receive Compliments

Now that we just discussed giving compliments, once you have mastered that move on to receiving compliments.

Receiving compliments is something that many struggles with.

Many people today are not use to giving or receiving compliments… especially woman! Here is a scenario of a perfect example of a compliment and the results.

Hi Sarah, "you look so beautiful today, and I just love that dress you are wearing."

Sarah response, "Really? This old dress, it's like 10 years old"….

How do you think the person that was giving the compliment felt?

Do you think that person would want to compliment Sarah again?

Exactly, All Sarah had to say was just … Thank you!

That is it. She did not ask her how long she had the dress for or any other details.

When someone says you are pretty, and you disagree, they are automatically going to think that person has low self-esteem in which many women do.

Daily, people attempt to give someone a compliment and instead of receiving it, they dismiss it.

Instead of being those people, or Sarah. Be the person that will accept compliments and appreciate the fact that someone went out there way to say something good to you.

Just simply say. Thank you! No matter if you feel what the person is saying is not true or you may not agree with them just accept the compliment and appreciate it.

There are many people out there wishing someone would compliment them, instead of seeing all the wrong they do. Some individuals' appearances are not up to par with what it should be and for years have not heard a single person acknowledge them. A compliment such as, you look amazing, will change how you can make them feel.

Be grateful and receive all good things into your life and a shift will happen. A question comes to mind.

What have you been thinking about?

You are what you attract.

The bible says in (***Psalms 23:7***) "As a man thinketh in his heart, so is he"

Whatever you are thinking about, is what you will manifest

You have manifested the life you are currently living and everything in it. The life you are living at this moment, you have created it with your thoughts.

Your thoughts are so powerful. Whatever you think of will come to past, whether if it is good or bad.

Stop and think for a moment:

- Your home

- Car

- Job

- Spouse

- The number of children you have

- If you're happy or not

- Your friends...etc.

You have more power over your lives than you think. What you focus on daily is what will come to past.

If you are a negative person and think of negative thoughts, you will attract more negativity in your life.

If you are a positive person and think of positive thoughts, you will attract more positivity in your life.

Do you know this saying?

"The rich get richer and the poor get poorer"- Anonymous-

It all goes back to *mindset*.

Rich people will focus on money and ways to multiply it, while poor people are constantly thinking about bills and spending their money.

You may get depressed because you think something outside of yourselves is keeping you from having what you want; however, what you are always thinking about is what will cause you to manifest your surroundings.

Power of Positive Thinking

Thinking positive will create a positive manifestation of your surroundings.

People tend to identify the negative in people and on people, than to see the positive.

Once you start to change your mindset, you will change your surroundings.

Change is affected by our subconscious mind and imagination. The bible talks about us being childlike. Children imaginations tend to go through the roof when you ask them what is on their minds. They do not hold on to grudge or jealousy. They will be mad at you for a moment and in less than 5 minutes, they are back to being your friend.

If adults will act more like children when it comes to imagination and seeing the good in all things, and not stressing over the things that are out of their control. They will be able to manifest an unstoppable mentality and start to attract positive things and people into their circle.

I know, I know… it's easier said, than done.

And yes, training your thoughts is not as easy as it sounds, but you have to start from somewhere.

Do the same thing over and over and expecting different results is the definition of being **insane**. No more doing the same thing over and over.

It is time for a change.

Training your thoughts is where it beings.

Waking up in the morning during the first 15 minutes, you're still operating in a portion of your subconscious mind.

    Be grateful

    Thinking only positive thoughts

    Seeing only good in others

Be friendly

Give compliments

Receive compliments

Think highly of yourself

Make a list of all of your accomplishments and what you are proud of!

Focus On What You Want!

Stop focusing your time on:

What you **don't** want?

What you **don't** like?

Whom you **don't** like?

What you **could** do better?

All the **negative** things others have said about you.

Bills, money, and things you **cannot** afford.

Instead, if you were to shift your thinking pattern to:

What you do want?

What you like?

Whom you like?

What you are proud of?

All the positive things others have said about you.

Be grateful for what you do have and research ways to make more money!

These steps are simple and very efficient. Take a moment and reflect on some good in your life.

Life does enough beating us down... For example, if you are not a specific weight, height, color then you are not good enough.

T.V doesn't help either. You have to come to a place of understanding that you are enough. This is how God made you and you need to accept yourself for who you are.

If there is something you are unhappy with and it's **in your control** to change it, by all means, change it.

If it's something **out of your control**, you cannot change leave it and do not dwell on it.

(Psalms 55:22) Cast your cares on the LORD and he will sustain you; he will never let the righteous be shaken.

Cast your cares on the Lord... He wants you to give him your burdens and let Him worry about them. He does not want you to carry the burden or fight the battle; it belongs to the Lord.

Stay focus on what you can control, change it and what we cannot control, give it God.

What Do You Value?

What is important to you? What do you value the most?

These questions are important to you if you want change in your life. Having clarity on your situation is the key to being clutter free.

Studies show that people that are messy spends more money than people who are clean. Clean people are usually organize and clear about what they want out of life.

The old saying that says,

"Cleanliness is next to Godliness" My mom would use this one on me over and over to keep my room clean while growing up.

Being clutter free allow you to see your situation for what it is,

Mental Declutter or Physical Declutter

Mental Declutter will allow you to declutter your mind body and soul. You will be more careful about what you do, listen to and what you watch. You will begin to understand the importance of what you do on a day to day will affect your mental state.

On the Other hand, **Physical Declutter** consist of your physical surroundings. The state of your home, workplace and even your vehicle. You may think this does not have much to do with gaining clarity, but it does. Studies show that an individual's space meaning home, workspace and vehicle is a reflection of their mind.

Cleaning your minds and cleaning your physical space will allow you to operate under clarity, which will enable you to be free in being able to prioritize what you want out of life.

Cleaning your mind and space will also allow you to operate out of a spirit of excellence.

In all you do, you want to do it to the best for your ability. In everything, operate in excellent.

Prioritize and gain clarity. Being clear on perfecting the best you is the key to you excelling forward. So many people can tell you everything they don't like and what they don't want, but never on what they do want..

One day I asked my sister,

Do you want to get to get married? Her response was, "Yes!"And then I asked, what type of husband do you want? She responded, "I don't want a husband with kids, with no job and do not want a husband that is out of shape."

I just looked at her and said, "That's not what I asked you"... She laughed and said, "You're right," and she went into deep thought and started to remove the "I do NOT want from her vocabulary. She thought long and hard about what she wanted and later that day she was able to answer the question that I had asked her. We had a great discussion and she was open to suggestions. She came in with an open mind, which allowed her to gain clarity on the type of husband she wanted.

In all things focus on what you want.

A famous pastor at church made an altar call... Hundreds of people came down. They all were praying and seeking the face of God.

He tapped a man on the shoulder and asked him, "What are you praying for?"

The man answered, "Nothing in particular." The Pastor told him, "That's exactly what you're going to get".

Be specific about what you want.

Be clear!

Remove your senseless thoughts, I do NOT want out of your vocabulary and start telling yourself and God what you truly WANT.

Notice I said yourself and God.

A famous book you may know called "The Little Red Book," has some basic principles in it that discuss how you need to speak to yourselves.

It's best to keep all of your dreams and goals to yourself until it begins to manifest.

As much as what you say is powerful, your thought is also compelling.

Be Yourself

You may think that you are not good enough and that you don't have anything to offer this world. You have all that you need inside of you to be and manifest all that you want out of life.

"Dare to be yourself, for we do that better than anyone else can" ~Anonymous

You can only be you. Stop trying to be someone else. You can just be great as yourself.

So many people put on a front and try to be someone they are not. Then they become stressed and uneasy because they are not living an authentic life.

Being true to who you are, will help you gain clarity during your walk through life.

Having a mentor or someone you look up to is okay but trying to be a person who you are really not is a No! No!

You want to assess the individual that you respect or look up to, but don't copy them,

Identify what it is they are doing differently that exude confidence and what you can learn from their actions. You can only be You!

> **You are enough!**
>
> **You are worth it!**
>
> **You can do it!**
>
> **Stay Focus!**
>
> **You got this!**

Be the Change You Want To See

Instead of waiting for others to change around you, be the change you want to see.

Stop telling others what they need to do and you start doing it first, and then others will follow.

There was a mom that told her children repeatedly do not smoke; however, the mom smoked one pack of Newport Cigarettes a day. The children then grew up and started to smoke one pack of cigarettes a day just like their mom. **Children will do what you do and not what you say.**

Be the example that you want to see, and others will follow.

People will follow your action than your words.

At one of the many jobs, I had a boss that will come in late every day. I mean like 11:30 am when the company will open at 8 am. Slowly but surely, the employees started to follow her. The goal was as long as they get in before her, they were good.

She decided to have a meeting and started to discuss the employee's time management and that she is disappointed in them. The employees in return told the boss but you come in late, we were trying to be more like you.

Again, we can tell people whatever we want but...

"Out action speaks louder than words"-Anonymous

Chapter 3
~Manifest Your Dreams~

WHAT IS YOUR FOUNDATION?

Take a moment and reflect on what is your foundation.

Do you have a solid foundation? Is your foundation weak? Is your foundation strong? Is your foundation built around money? If you do not have any money, do you feel worthless? Is your foundation built on relationship? If you are not in a relationship, do you feel alone? What is your foundation or whom is your foundation?

God needs to be your foundation regardless of any situation. Your foundation has to be something greater than you are. Think of a building or even a Skyscraper, its foundation has to strong or else it cannot stand.

You should think of yourselves the same. The higher you go the more stable your foundation needs to be. What does that mean? You need to redefine your relationship with the Lord as you grow.

People tend to do the complete opposite, the more they achieve, the less and less they depend on God.

It's mentioned three times in the bible

(Matthew 19:24, Mark 10:25 & Luke 18:25) For it is easier for a camel to go through the eye of a needle than for a rich person to enter the Kingdom of God.

What Jesus was implying was not the physical but from a spiritual standpoint. An example would be:

Wealthy people sometimes typically feel like they don't need God when things or events are going good because they think it's all them who built their fortune. However, that is not true! You may feel successful and see success, but as fast as your wealth accumulates, is as fast as it can go...

How many times have you turned on the T.V. and a wealthy person committed suicide? A number of wealthy people are unhappy and feel lonely. Remember, it does not matter if you are rich or poor; your foundation has to be solid in Christ.

What Jesus was implying is that you should, in all things depend on your Lord and Savior.

Constantly Educate Yourself

Education is Key! We have heard that so many times growing up. Yes, I do agree that education is vital but what form of education are you talking about?

Does education mean anything to you, if it's on a topic or a subject that you will never use or discuss ever in life?

Educate yourself and seek *personal self-development!*

Yes, you can educate yourself on new topics and subjects, but what good would it be if you were lacking education in the most important part of your life. Gaining knowledge in an area that is less important will increase your awareness.

For example: if you wanted to gain Financial Freedom, you should be educating yourself by researching financial literacy using books, video, documentary, etc. on financial freedom.

If you want to gain confidence, you should be reading books, watching videos on gaining confidence and surrounding yourself with people that are confident and fully motivated.

Do your research!

If you continue to read those same Love books instead of reading a Financial Literacy books, how do you plan to gain the financial information you need?

Seek those who are on the same motivated path as you and study their patterns for success.

Start looking into what they do and how they did it and make it your duty to incorporate their steps to success in your plan.

"Success Leave Clues" - Tony Robbins

Faith

Having faith in others is easier said than done. You will have to trust that person fully. Unfortunately, people are known for continually disappointing each other. Especially, in today's society, many people find it hard to trust each other.

Faith- complete trust or confidence in someone or something. Faith in yourself and faith in God.

Having faith in others is not bad, but expect disappointments. If you shift that process of depending on others and start depending on yourself, meaning to trust yourself fully and put your faith in God,

Many people have faith in God and none in themselves. You have to build up faith in yourself as well. The Lord is the head of all you do and it is your job to worship and praise your Lord and Savior. God also wants us to do some "work" and feel confident.

(**James 2:26**) For as the body without the spirit is dead, so faith without works is dead.

Putting in *WORK* is just as important as having faith.

A man named Steve decided he was tired of being home and wanted to find a job. It has been three years since he worked. Steve has been in church all his life and decided he will take a leap of faith. Steve decided that he would have faith that one day he will get a job. He focused on having a job night and day, months went by and nothing happened. He prayed about it repeatedly and still no change. Not once did Steve go online and fill out an application. That would have been his *"WORK"*. He just thought by praying and believing that was enough, he had to put in the work.

If Steve would have completed applications, went to different companies with his resume and asked around, then a job or many jobs would have become available to him.

Apparently, Steve thought someone was going to knock on his door and ask if he was looking for a job. Really Steve!

You have to put in the work. I am not saying miracles cannot happen, absolutely it can. Putting in the work is what will complete your faith walk.

Having the mindset and praying is not enough, you have to put in the *WORK*.

A lady by the name Shay wanted to lose weight. Shay wanted to lose 40 pounds. She was tired of looking the way she did and wanted a change. Shays eating habits consisted of coffee, donuts, hamburgers, fries, brownies, and fast food for dinner. With this type of diet, we both know that losing 40 pounds will be hard unless she makes a change. Shay decided she needed help and will pray about being slim. She prayed to God every morning and night about losing the 40 pounds, she continued to eat the same way repeatedly. She heard a woman at work say, not only should she pray, she should think about losing weight as much as possible. Shay did that for about 2 months and still no change. When she got on the scale, it showed she had gained an additional 5 pounds. Shay was so discouraged. At this point, her faith had decreased and her mindset was wavering. She continued to pray but this time she began to look up healthy recipes and she started working out. She started to put in "*WORK*"! Shay was determined to lose which was now 45 pounds instead of 40 because she gained the additional 5 pounds. She was consistent. She prayed, she had a positive mindset, ate healthy and worked out daily for 1 hour. Shay was able to lose 58 pounds. Exceeding her expectation.

(***Hebrew 11:1***)Now faith is the substance of things hoped for, evidence of things not seen.

Putting in "*WORK*" will save you time, energy and heartache. People just want to sit back and let God do all the work. God is looking at you saying, "If you have to put in some work, I will meet you halfway."

Follow the simple Nuggets:

- Have Faith

- Pray Everyday

- Have a Positive Mindset

- Put in the **WORK**!

God can do all things, but as his children you have to stop being so lackadaisical, and full of excuses. You expect God to do it all for you, NOT! You have to put in some work.

Your Cup Running Over
Your cup means-what is in you?

Many people walk around for days, months & years with nothing in their cup. That is like wanting to drive to a different state, but your car gas is always on E (Empty).

Is this You?

How could you be a blessing to someone when you do not have anything to give?

How could you pour out to others when you have nothing inside of you? This is why you may be stressed out?

Your cup may be running low or on empty.

Some of us only put $10 worth of gas in our tank knowing by tomorrow we need to get more gas. Every day we will have to put more in our tank to get around. That is like wanting more but refusing to change the situation to get more out of life.

Is it better to fill up and allow what you have to carry you through the week? Than to go back and fill up again everyday. Or should you fill up your cup and let it overflow and what's running over is what you pour unto others?

You have to fill up your cup. Not a little at a time... Not just enough to carry us through the week.... Fill up to the point that your cup is running over.

Only what's running over is what you can give to others. You can pour into them when you have something to give.

When you pour into others while you are empty, you feel burnt out. The key is never get burnt out. You have to continue going back to the source and get refilled.

What good is a phone that is on 3%, while on a call?

What good is a car on E (empty) when you're about to get on the road and start a journey from Florida to New York?

What good is a person with an empty cup trying to pour into others?

What do you have to give?

Giving is the source of your solution.

Getting filled up and staying filled up will allow you to get through life feeling complete.

A woman was in the kitchen making toast for breakfast. She places the bread in the toaster and pushes down the handle. She waited and waited but nothing happened. She started touching the toaster. Then she put her hand over the toaster to check if it was getting hot, but nothing. She realized that the toaster was never plugged in.

You will never be able to perform at your best unless you are plugged into the source. That thing that gives you strength.

(*Nehemiah 8:10*) The joy of the Lord is my strength.

(*Psalm 28:7*) The Lord is my strength and shield.

The Lord is that source you need to perform at your best. When you are plugged in he will protect you, strengthen and give you joy.

To perform at your best you need the Lord to fill you up until you overflow. The goal is to be so in tune with the Lord to the point that you have so much inside of you. When you pour into others, you stay filled.

You can tell when someone is filled.

They're usually the ones that are enjoying life. Obstacles still come their way but they don't allow it to affect them. They handle things differently from someone who is empty.

Empty people are usually always on the verge of giving up, easily offended and easily distracted. Their distractions are greater than their dreams, and desires.

Allow the Lord to strengthen you.

Prayer time is important. You have to spend time with God. So many people speak of God, but don't speak to God. You need to get to know God for yourself. Don't take what others say. Not even what your Pastor. You need to spend time with God and get to know him for yourself.

Being in the presence of God is the best thing that you can do. You need some time with Him. God is talking to you, but can you hear Him? Or are you too busy to hear Him?

Manifest Your Dreams

Stop living life for others and start living for yourself.

>What makes you happy?

>What makes you smile?

>What are your dreams?

>What are your goals?

These are things that some of us can't even answer because we have no clue.

Life has beaten us up so much to the point that we don't even know what makes us smile. Live and gain your happiness. If you have dreams, pursue them! If you have goals, achieve them.

Stop making excuses and go after what you want in life. Life is too short not to be happy. Someone is in a worst situation than you are. Be grateful for what you have and where you are.

Protect your dreams. Stop allowing others to tell you how to dream and what to dream. Stop being obligated to others and *START* being obligated to your dreams.

When an employee starts a new job, the employer always expresses to the employee their job description, benefits, expectation, and schedule.

Also, the employer expresses a 90-day probation. If you're anything like me, I will be fully committed to those 90 days so after that I can reap the benefits.

The job will say don't be late, do this, do that and have the highest expectations for the employee and people will do it.

Let's say after the 90 days, you learn that the job does not have any benefits, insurance, 401k, or vacation time. How would you feel? During the interviewing process, the employer assured you of all the benefits you were going to get.

At this point, you will no longer want to work for the company because of false advertising. They said they were going to do something but reneged. We as people take other people words very seriously. We will quit the job, walk over to the manager and say, "Sorry, I can not settle for this job," especially if we had expectations and the employer did not hold up their side of the agreement. We will even go as far as re-reading the employee handbook over and over looking for some information that may change the situation. Some of us may even want to sue because of the inaccurate information the company was offering.

Why don't we take our *Dreams* that serious?

Many people want others around them to be true to their word and be as honest as possible. If someone says they will do something, you will be sure that they it get done. Are you like that? When it comes to your dreams and goals are you that person? Do you hold yourself accountable when you don't pull through?

Do you promise yourself things and don't follow through? You should hold yourself accountable for not following through on the things you promise yourself. When you promise yourself something, you should do everything in your power to get it completed.

You have to stop giving up on your Dreams.

Your dream are uniquely created for you. No one else, just you.

Many may have something similar, but it's not the same.

You have to get to a place and say enough is enough. I am going to accomplish my goals and dreams. Put a deadline on it.

By this year..... I will accomplish this list of things.

Hold yourself to it. Many are so loyal to companies and friend but never loyal to themselves.

>Be obligated to yourself

>Be obligated to your dreams

>Hold yourself accountable

>Once you have accomplished your dreams. **Reward yourself!**

Dreamers Take Action and Move Forward!

Some of you are *dreamers*, meaning God has reveals things to you in your dreams. Some of you receive visions and some of you hear the voice of God

When God reveals visions to you, He gives it to you with the expectations that you will carry out this vision or what you heard the Lord say.

(***Isaiah 55:11***) God word never return to Him void.

When God says or shows you something, it must come to past. Whether it's something big or something small.

Get out of your own way and take action.

Dreamers take action! Dreamers do not sit back and wait for things to happen. Dreamers get up and create a plan.

Timeout for excuses.

The time is now!

Now is the time. Stop putting your dreams and goals off.

Stop saying, I will wait until next year. Stop acting as though your dreams are not that important.

Your dreams are extremely *important* and it's YOUR JOB to see to it that your dreams and goals are fully accomplished.

How to Handle Negative People?

Negative people will always have something to say. It is not your job to correct them. Negative people are only negative because their lives are a living hell. They are unhappy in their lives and it's filled with all kind of jealousy, envy and hurt.

It is not your job to correct them or tell them a piece of your mind. Just refrain from associating yourself with them.

Your space needs to be sacred. You cannot operate in the spirit when negative people are draining your positive energy.

Have you ever allowed a negative person to associate themselves with you and the little time they were in your presence they made your whole mood change?

The best way to deal with negative people is not to deal with them at all.

What if the negative person is your spouse, child or a close friend?

It is your job to stay as prayed up as possible and always exude positivity. Over-shadow them with love and speak only positive things out of your mouth.

In the beginning, they will feel annoyed, but eventually, they will appreciate hearing positive things.

Then their words will change and they will start to say things like: "Wow, you are like a breath of fresh air" and that is the goal. In the beginning, there will be a fight between the two energies positive and negative, love always conquers all.

How to Handle Negative Thoughts

Negative thought will arise. Even if you are the most positive person. Even down to your spiritual leaders, have negative thoughts.

The way to deal with a negative thought is when it comes, dismiss it.

Meaning when you are sitting there meditating or just thinking about all the good things in life, then the enemy shows up and you start hearing or seeing negative things, just dismiss it and cancel it.

When I first started my *positive thoughts only* Journey, it was very hard in the beginning because it felt like it was impossible to train your thoughts. As the time went on, I started to learn how to train my thoughts and when one negative thought slipped through, I would do a physical act to remove it.

I use to shake my head, as if I am saying No and say, "I cancel you in the name of Jesus." I continued this saying until I did not have to physically say it anymore. I will mentally say it.

Your Dreams Needs to Exceed Your Reality

If your dreams do not exceed your reality, go back and try again.

Your dreams are supposed to EXCEED your reality. You have to fight for your greatness. Don't let your light dim for anyone. You are who you are for a reason.

Your dreams and goals should scare you. It should make you nervous. It should make you want to hide. It should make you feel like God gave it to the wrong person. Your dreams and goals should also make you feel like it's impossible to achieve, you don't have the ability to do it.

If you don't feel this way you have to go back and try once more. It should make you fearful. When you feel this way, you are on the right path. You need to understand that your dreams and goals are waiting on YOU to be executed. However, even though you may feel this way the reality is that you have it in you, to accomplish your dreams and you will. No one else, but you can do it.

Chapter 4
~*Who's In Your Circle*~

YOUR CIRCLE

Who is in your circle? Who are you surrounded by? Who do you spend most of your time with?

"Show me your friends, and I will tell you who you are." - Anonymous

Your circle is a representation of you. Take a moment and think of who you spend most of your time with? Are they super positive, motivating and empowering? Or, are the people in your circle negative, stressed and depressed?

Think about the circle you currently have and the amount of money they are now making. Is that the amount of money you desire to make?

Studies show that people who make a $1 more or less than the people they tend to stay around. I'm not telling to ditch your friends but I'm telling you if you want to reach a particular place financially you may want to consider having friends in a different tax bracket.

You may think yeah, they may be negative, but you're not. I can assure you somewhere in your life you are similar to the people in your circle.

If you want change, you have to become the change you want to see. You have to surround yourself with positive, motivating and empowering people if that is what you want to become.

You are what you attract.

Your circle needs to be sacred. You need to be around people that care about your wellbeing and will uplift and inspire you to do and be better.

Surround yourself with positivity. It is so easy to fall in negativity or gossip. You have to be the change. Do not allow others to take up space in your mind or space that cannot help you become a better you.

When I use to work for this company. I meet four amazing co-workers. Out of the four, two of them had a very negative disposition. I tried to always motivate them and tell them to think positive. They had reached a point that if they had something negative to say, they will no longer tell me because they knew I would redirect the conversation. They stopped coming to me with all the negative issues they were having and started to tell me only the good things. I did not stop talking to them. We kept our friendship, but they will always tell me only the positive, uplifting and empowering stories. The other stories, they kept it among themselves.

You may think you cannot change others, which in reality you cannot, but you can change yourself, shift the atmosphere and watch, like attract like.

Gratitude

The quality of being grateful or thankful.

This is a form of giving. Give thanks for everything. Be grateful for what you have. Stop worrying about what you do not have and start thanking God for what you do have.

Give thanks in all circumstances, this is God's Will for you in Christ Jesus.

Focusing on what you *do not* have or what you *should* have is only going to make you feel horrible. It will make you feel like you are not worth anything.

This is not what God wants for you. He wants us to have the best; however, always complaining or worrying is not going to bring what you want any sooner.

What will bring those things that we desire is being *grateful*.

In all things, give thanks.

(Psalms 100:4) Enter His gates with thanksgiving and His courts with praise, give thanks to Him and praise His name. Entering into Gods courts, He wants us to come with thanksgiving.

First, ask God for forgiveness and then thank God for everything. He does not want you coming to him complaining, begging, or worrying. He wants you to come to him with thanksgiving and being grateful for everything you have.

Think about it for a second. Many people complain about the silliest things in life, when there are people that have lost their lives and some who are fighting for their lives. Instead of them being grateful they are alive and their children are alive.

God wants to bless you.

He is just waiting for you to shift your mindset and start to thank Him and be grateful for all that you have. Watch and see God bless you.

Be thankful, grateful and appreciate what you have because someone has it 10 times worse than you do.

Do Better!

In order to get better, you have to do better.

You must always grow in all areas of your life. Doing the same thing repeatedly and expecting a different result is the definition of being insane.

You say to yourself that you want grow in a particular area in your life. If you want to grow in an area then try your best, take ownership, and create better habits.

If you feel like your money is tight and you want to save instead of buying lunch every day, bring lunch from home and save money. If you do not bring your lunch, think about it! It's $10 day, $200 a month, and $2400 a year. In the beginning, it may not sound like much but it does add up. Start saving your lunch money so you can increase your savings.

People have a tendency to feel stuck. You no longer have to feel stuck. If you do not like something, change it. If you are tired of being overweight then stop eating all that unnecessary food and instead workout and eat healthily.

What I am trying to advocate is that, you have the power within you to do better instead of complaining about and feeling stuck. You can do it.

Prayer Changes Things

Complaining vs Prayer. *Prayer* will always be in the lead. However, as humans, our first instinct is to be negative.

Complaining will get you nowhere. If you pray about your situation and leave it to God. Watch and see God work.

(*2 Chronicles 7:14*) If my people, who are called by my name, will humble themselves and pray and seek my face and turn from their wicked ways, then I will hear from heaven, and I will forgive their sin and will heal their land.

If you want God to hear you, you must humble yourselves and pray about it.

You cannot pray, worry and complain. It is either you worry and complain or you pray and leave it to God.

Believe In What You Pray For

God wants you to go to Him in spirit and in truth. You have to believe in what you pray for. You have to walk with a spirit of expectancy.

Knowing that once you have completed your prayer, count it as done. You are now expecting God to do it for you.

It's as simple as going to work. When you go to work after 2 weeks you are now *expecting* your paycheck. You don't have to ask any questions or second guess about if or when your check is arriving, you already know when it's coming and the amount you will receive. You're walking in *expectancy* knowing that the money will be deposited in your account because you put in the *work*.

Prayer is the work. When you put in the work, there is no need to beg, cry or wonder. You know for a fact that your paycheck will be there and that's the same expectancy you should have once you have giving it to God.

You don't have to second guess or feel like you are not sure or maybe God won't do it for you. God wants to do it for you. He wants you to have an abundant life. He wants to provide you with all that you have asked for. It is your job to put in the work and pray *without ceasing*.

Give everything to God. He needs to be in the midst of everything that you do. Prayer is powerful. Once you prayed, believed that God will do it for you, put in the work, walk with expectancy. Watch and see Him do it.

Stop Believing Others

Over the years, people have said so many negative things about you. Yes, some have said positive things, but unfortunately the negativity remarks are ones that's remembered the most. If someone mention something negative over your life **cancel it**. Don't believe the negative remarks. They will tell you what they think looks nice on you. What color they want you to do your hair. They will even tell you what they DON'T like about you.

No, you should wear that!

Why would you want to go back to school?

You are going to be at this job forever!

You will never be rich!

Don't believe what they say, believe what God says about you!

You can wear that!

You can further your education!

You will be promoted to a new position!

Your millions are waiting on you!

Stop letting people dictate who you are and what you can accomplish. If you want it, ***it's yours***. You have to understand that you can and will do *All* things through Christ who strengthens you.

You can do all and you will do *All* the things that your heart desires. **Stay focus!**

Believe In Your Dream

Your dreams can be accomplished. You have to believe that it can. You can't get these amazing dreams and then sit on them. Do not even start second-guessing yourself. You have to believe that your dreams can be accomplished. As a matter of fact, you need to put a deadline on your dreams. Jot it down!

(*Habakkuk 2:2*) And the LORD answered me: "Write the vision; make it plain on tablets.

Be clear about what you want and write it down. No matter how big it sounds.. A great book I read, mention for us to follow these simple steps when it comes to believing in your dreams and goals:

Write It Down

Read it over 3x a day (Morning, Noon & Night).

Tell no one!

Not telling anyone is super important. If you're anything like me, when I get a vision or God shows me something that's Amazing! The first thing I do is thank God of course. The second thing is, to get on the phone and call someone, I automatically tell them what God told me. God did not give them the vision. He gave the vision to you! The person who you told may respond as though they care or they get it, but in actuality they may be thinking to themselves or say out of their mouth, there is no way you can get this done. That discouraging attitude is not needed while executing your vision.

This is why it is super important for you to not only write it down, read it over and over, *do not to tell anyone*. I know it's hard.

I think it's one of the most challenging step to follow. Not everyone wants to see you succeed. Not even family. Sometimes, family and your closest friends are the ones that will hurt you the most and kill your dreams by their negative feedback and thoughts.

Instead of talking about it.... Accomplish it and watch all of those naysayers.

Whatever you think, you can hold in your hand. Whatever you want out of life go for it. Life is too short for you not to. You have only one life to live so make it count.

You can have anything that you think about. If you really want it, you can get it. Don't allow anyone to tell you what you can and can't have. You can accomplish anything you put your mind to.

Chapter 5
~*Renew Your Mind*~

MINDSET

"Change your mind, Change your life"

Don't underestimate the power that God has given you. God created you like him.

(*Genesis 1:27*) You can create a negative, miserable and dramatic life for yourself, or you can create a happy, joyous and meaningful life. Create your world means to create your own reality.

God has given you the ability to Co-create just like he did when creating the world that we live in.

If you are created in his image, that means you can do what God does. Now, we know we cannot create on the magnitude like God did, but we can on this earth because God gave us dominion over this world.

If you don't like the hand you were dealt then go back to the dealer and get a new one.

How many times have you heard people that came from nothing, were able to get a new hand dealt and now they live the life that they have always desired? You have the ability to create a better life for yourself.

You have to understand the power that God gave you. If you want to be better, you have to do better.

If you are constantly put in the atmosphere, "I will never be rich", you will get just that. You will never be rich.

If you are always speaking down to yourself and others around you, you will always be in a negative state of mind.

If you speak positivity out of your mouth then you will receive just that.

What you say out of your mouth will manifest whether it is good or bad, positive or negative. God will allow what you think to come to past.

What are you thinking about consistently?

Are you thinking positive thoughts most of the time?

Or, are negative thoughts consuming your time and space?

Have you ever been in a classroom setting and the teacher gets up and asks a question and you think to yourself "don't call on me, don't call on me." and the teacher calls on you?

God gave you dominion over this earth. Contrary to popular belief, the laws of the land are still in full effect. What you ask for is what you will get. Just remember, what you think about is what will come to past.

Shifting your mindset is a must if you want to see different results. Always thinking negative and speaking negatively will result in you living a negative life.

What you think in your heart will also manifest.

(***Proverbs 23:7***) As a man thinketh in his heart so is he.

You are what you think about. So what are you thinking about?

It's not difficult, it's actually very simple. The power of the tongue speaks death or life. What are you speaking out of your mouth?

(***Proverbs 18:21***) Death and life are in the power of the tongue.

Meaning that you have the power to speak life into yourselves.

Someone who I recently have spoken with, told me that she was diagnosed with cancer. She told me that most of the women in her family were diagnosed with cancer. She also mentioned to me that she *knew* she was going to get it, she just didn't know when.

I was so shocked to hear her say that because I thought to myself …. She *knew*?

Just because someone in your family have gone through rough times or illnesses, doesn't mean that you will receive it or it will happen to you. You could have been the special one that the cancer decided to jump right over because you believe in your heart that you are healed.

I just started to think about others that are diagnosed. Did they think it or speak the sickness into their lives?

It may sound crazy, but the bible says death and life are in the power of the tongue. So the answer to that is, yes! Some of them did speak sickness, pain, hurt in their lives.

Yes, horrible things happen to good people. I have heard many people diagnosis themselves with disease. Disease comes from your body is no longer at ease. Many people are suffering in their bodies because of what they have spoken over their lives and over other people lives.

What about those who are living an abundant life. The speak positivity, think positive thoughts, they focus on the word of God, prayer, exercising and eating clean. Those people are so focused on being healthy mentally, physically and emotionally that they don't allow any negativity to consume them and contaminate their body or space.

Take some time and think about your life for a minute.

You have co-created the life you are currently living whether it's good or bad.

- Home
- Car
- Job
- Salary
- Health and everything else.
- Are you happy with what you have Co-created?
- Do you want a change?

I remember the first time I realized that I co-created my life, I was torn. I couldn't believe it. Being so unhappy, lonely, broke, overweight, lived in a horrible neighborhood and just miserable.

Hated my job and disliked my co-workers. Thinking to myself, there's no way I could love myself by allowing my situation to get the best of me.

I didn't know any better. Nobody never taught this to me. I told myself I had to do better. I started reading books, listening to audios, watching video on how to improve my mindset and my life. Many years later, here I am sharing this gift with you.

It may seem like a lot in the beginning, but I will assure you that it will be all worth it in the end.

One of the things that got me going is repetition.

I had to do things that others won't, to live the life that others don't.

I stop listening to senseless gestures and started to see my eyes and ears as a gateway. I started to realize how powerful words can be when spoken into the atmosphere. I became more alert and careful about what I spoke out of my mouth.

Affirmations

The action or process of affirming something or being affirmed.

When was the last time you affirmed something?

Affirming something in your lives may seem difficult, but it's not.

"Sticks and stones may break my bones but words will never hurt me"~ Anonymous

If you are anything like me, as much as this sounds great, we both know that words can hurt you.

People will always have something negative to say to stop you from feeling great or moving towards your destination. They will always identify all of your flaws. You must not indulge in negative conversation or small talk because remember whatever you speak into the atmosphere will most likely manifest. Be careful!

When was the last time you said something good about yourself?

If people constantly speak negative, who is going behind them and reversing every ill spoken word over their life.

One day I was mentoring a group of middle school kids and we started talking about Affirmations. I explained to them how powerful words are. I showed the following *Exercise*

Bowl Exercise

Bowl 1 - Reflects all the **negative** things that people have said about them.

All the negative things! What their mom, dad, teacher, friend, and anyone else we thought of had that have said anything negative about them. There was a bowl with balls and the balls represented negative words. As you already know, this bowl was overflowing with about 25 balls.

Bowl 2- Reflects all the **positive** things that people have said about them

All the positive things! Compliments, encouragement and nice things of what mom, dad, teacher, friends and anyone else we could have thought of. In this bowl, there was about 3- 4 balls representing the number of positive words.

These kids were shocked. If we are co-creators like we discussed earlier, then why do we allow others to create our world? We allow others to speak things over our lives when we have the power to speak things into our own lives as many times a day as possible.

After the bowl exercise...............

When you first start with your Affirmation it may feel funny especially if you have never done it before. As you continue to do it, it will start to unveil the power of your words.

Look into who you are and what you want to be and start speaking these things over your life.

Create a list. List all the things that you desire to be and what you think of yourself.

List-

1. *I AM* Beautiful - you may not currently feel like you are beautiful but this is a desire of where you want to be or feel.

If you're not the great of a cook... Your List should say.

2. *I AM* a great cook

These are just examples of how you will create your list of positive words that you will like to establish in your life.

Now, make your List..... Here's an example of my list when I first got started.

>*I AM* a Mighty woman of God
>
>*I AM* an Amazing mother
>
>*I AM* an Incredible wife
>
>*I AM* the head and not the tail
>
>*I AM* above and not beneath
>
>*I AM* a Best Selling Author
>
>*I AM* Wealthy
>
>*I AM* Healthy
>
>*I Can* do All thing through Christ who strengthens me

During this exercise, DO NOT listen to anyone else opinion about you. This list needs to reflect what you think about you, what God says about you and where you desire to be. Stop looking for others Approval. Only approval you need is God!

After establishing your list, if we were to go back to the bowl exercise, the negative words others have spoken over your life that was in bowl

1 and bowl 2 had the positive words, would it made a difference? How do you think it will play out?

After Affirming who you are and whose you are, you will become those examples and things will look a little different.

Bowl Exercise 2

Bowl 1

Negative words that was about to overflow.

Bowl 2

Positive words... I AM....

We don't have to wait on others to provide us with positive words because we can speak positivity over our own life..... and fill up the bowl with positive words.

Your affirmation needs to be established every day and repeated daily.

Repetition is powerful! Doing it first thing in the morning will start to reflect in your subconscious mind.

Why daily? Because every day it should be your desire to create a better life for yourself.

Affirming who you are on a daily basis will cancel out all the negative words that others may have spoken or even have thought in their minds about you.

Reap What You Sow

What are you sowing? You may have heard this saying so many times, but no one discusses what they are sowing. Everyone wants to reap the benefits but don't want to put in the work.

Putting in the work is how you will reap, whether it's, praying and fasting to gain a deeper connection with God, or working out and eating healthy to live a healthier life

Sowing reminds me of Karma. What you put out is what you will get in return!

Everyone wants to live an amazing wealthy lifestyle with all the money, cars and mansion. However, when individuals see the amount of sowing/work those individuals put in they no longer want that lifestyle anymore because it's a lot of work.

What have you sown?

It's just as simple as giving back, whether it's paying tithes, blessing others that are less fortunate or giving to a charity.

Every big corporation have a charity that they give back to whether they believe in God or not. Giving back is another *law of the land*. You will reap whether you are a Christian or not. This is something that has been established before Christianity was formed.

When was the last time you gave?

People have a tendency to not give. When they get their pay they want to hold onto it and the key to prosperity is you have to give a portion back.

This is a necessity if you what to reap. You have to sow a seed in order for that seed to grow so it can bear fruit.

Many people don't want to sow, but they want to reap a harvest. That's like you going over to a seed that was never placed into the soil, water it and waiting for it to flourish. How will it flourish if you have never sown a seed? It will never grow because the seed was never placed in soil to grow.

This may be a hard pill to swallow; however, this is important and if we don't *give,* as the bible says, we are robbing God.

(Malachi 3:8) Will a man rob God? Yet you are robbing me. But you say, 'How have we robbed you?' In your tithes and contributions.

Yes, it is possible that we can rob God by not giving our tithes and offering.

In All Things See the Good

If you were to look at your surroundings, you will be able to notice so many things that you don't like. I want you to take that same look around and start thinking about all the things you do like.

It's time now to stop focusing on all the negative that surrounds you and start paying attention to all of the positive. In all things, see the good.

See good in people, situation and every obstacle that comes up.

Some people are programmed to think objectively. "Oh no, what now"? Or, what's the worst that can happen?

Instead of them saying, "Lord, why me", began to saying "Thank You God. It could've been worst."

People need to let go of the negative state of mind and start recognizing that someone out there is in a worst situation than them. Be grateful!

Start enjoying the people and things that are around you. Start looking at things differently. When you wake up, take a moment, smell the roses, enjoy where you are in life and who you are in life.

No, you may not be where you want to be, but you're not where you use to be and remember the best is yet to come.

Be grateful for the little things.

Live Life to the Fullest

This is your life. No one else can live it for you. Every day you wake up, God has given you another chance to be great and to chase your dreams. Stop taking life for granted. People are dying every day and before you leave this earth, you need to make the best of your situation.

Stop looking for others to make you happy. Happiness starts from within. Only you can truly make you happy.

Start living your life, how you want it to be. Do something different each day.

> Start listening to music
>
> Plan a date with your spouse, if you haven't gone out in a while
>
> Change your hair
>
> Wear something different.
>
> Take a different route to work
>
> Get a membership at a gym
>
> Try a new restaurant
>
> Go to networking events
>
> Meet new people

Get out of that boring cycle of things and start to change your routine.

You have to do something different to get a different outcome. Life is too short to be old and miserable. Enjoy the moment and everyone around you.

Start smiling and embracing the person that God has created, which is YOU!

How to Start Your Morning

The way you start your morning have an effect on the rest of your day. Starting your morning right will set the tone for the rest of your day.

The **power hour** is the first hour of the morning which is also the most powerful hour of your day.

Most people morning start off rough. Their alarm will go off, and they make the decision to go back to sleep and get a little more rest. When they do decide to wake up, they're now running late. They spent their morning running around trying to gather all that they need for work. When they finally get on the road, they are utterly driving like a maniac. Everyone else is driving the speed limit and they're the only one in a rush. Now, they get to work a couple of minutes late and forgot they had an important meeting in the morning with the executive boss.

That scenario sounds like a lot of people I know. The art of being on time says a lot about an individual.

Taking control of your morning starts with you getting a good night's rest. Going to bed 4 am and waking up 6 am is not the ideal rest that your body needs.

Go to bed on time. Give yourself time to rest and allow your body to recover from a day's work. This power hour can be changed to fit your schedule. Customize it and make it your own.

The three primary focus is your ***mind, body***, and ***spirit***. These are the three things that people are always trying to better. But one needs the other. Just increasing your body and not your mind is a waste. Here are the keys to starting your morning:

Power Hour keeps you motivated!

The first 20 minutes consist of prayer, spending time with God. Telling God thank you for waking you up in the morning and focusing on the things you are grateful for. The attitude of gratitude, spending time seeing yourself being that amazing person you want to be, and spending a moment to reflect on how you will feel if you were living that amazing life that you desire.

The second 20 minutes consist of reading, empowering and educating your mind. This may be spent by you reading the bible, a book that will help increase areas in your life that you will like to work on or an audio that you will listen to that will help motivate and inspire you. This will help stimulate your mind and get you ready to start your day.

The last 20 minutes will consist of you working out or doing some form of a physical activity. You can go for a walk or do something that will get your blood flowing. This one is important because you will get your physical work out and get your energy level increased. This will be a light form of physical activity to clear your mind and get you ready to start your day.

Once your power hour is completed, you may begin your day.

You Are, What You Say

Whatever you say, is usually a reflection of who you are. When was the last time you said something positive about yourself?

People that have self-doubt normally has low self-esteem. People who speak highly of themselves normally are confident individuals.

You have to get to the place in your life where you stop speaking as though you are disguised with who you are and start taking pride in yourself.

What are you saying about yourself?

Speak Life into Yourself

Speaking life into yourself is key to self-love. Stop waiting on others to tell you and start telling yourself. You are amazing and you can do it!

You have to start looking in the mirror and start speaking to that person that you see.

If you had an opportunity to tell the younger you what to do, what will you tell the younger you?

If you're visited by a more attractive, vibrant, successful and confident version of you, a version of who you desired to be. What would they want to tell you?

Everything is going to be okay! You can do it! Don't be afraid! You have to get in the habit of speaking life into yourself, meaning speaking great thing to yourself. It's okay to speak to yourself. You are beautiful and amazing and never forget that

Love Yourself

"If you love yourself then others will follow" -Anonymous-

People treat you how you treat yourself.

If you love yourselves, you are showing people an example of how to treat you. You first have to do it for others to follow. Women may want a man to love them, but they do not love themselves. So what's going to happen, the man is going to treat the woman the same way how she treats herself.

If you are always cheap with yourselves, your significant other will be cheap with you. If you like the expensive things, he/she will know that this is what he/she wants and will get it for him/ her.

You are the firsthand - example of how you want others - to treat you.

Spend a little time reflecting on how you treat yourself.

Is it how you will like others to treat you?

Is this an area you need to work on?

Treat others how you want to be treated. Treat *yourself* how you want others to treat *you*.

CHAPTER 6
~*SILENCE*~

IMPORTANCE OF SILENCE & MEDITATION

This generation of people today are always busy and on the move. They are always focused on their next move and their busy long to-do list they have created.

All day they are just going and going and going. They get in the car they have to make phone calls and when they reach a red light, they are texting and trying to send an email. Continuous!

The constant multitasking, which may seem like an advantage to you, or thinking that you are being super productive but in actuality, the excessive simulation does not allow you to perform at your best.

Operate in excellence: however, doing seven things at once will not allow you to do it to the best of your ability.

"Jack of all trades, master of none" - Anonymous-

Sounds familiar!

In all things, do it to the best of your ability, but give yourself time to do these activities.

> After working all day, do you take a moment and reflect?
>
> Do you have any quiet time?
>
> Do you have time for God?
>
> Do you have time to spend with yourself?

Quiet time may consist of prayer, private meditation, and worship of God or spending time with God.

People want to receive all the blessings and all the good things, but have no time to spend it with the creator. God wants to bless you with all good things, but you have no time for him.

Spend Time with God

Spending time with God will give you freedom, unspeakable joy, and spiritual maturity. You will also gain discipline, stability, and purpose.

If you have ever questioned what is your purpose, spend time with your creator, and He will direct your path. God will reveal things to you during the quiet time with him.

The Lord loves when his children spend time with him. Wouldn't you want your children to spend time with you?

Many people think they know God because they said their Grace before they ate, or the two hours they spent in the church not listen because they are scrolling through their social media on their phones. Last night before they went to sleep they said, "Thank you, Lord."

Is that enough?

God is speaking. Can you hear Him? Or, is your schedule too busy to hear Him?

During your quiet time with God, He speaks. Many people say they never heard God's voice and the reason is they can't hear Him is because they are too busy.

God wants to be in all things that we do. He wants us to come to Him for everything. People like to pick the problems they want to God fix. For example, Hmmmmm, I'm going to take this one on myself, but that one, I'm going to give that to God… **That's not what God wants**…

(*Psalm 55:22*)

Give your burdens to the LORD, and he will take care of you. He will not permit the godly to slip and fall.

God wants you to give every burden, situation, and issue you have, to Him.

Seek God and all things will be added. He will give you your heart's desire, if you spend time with Him.

Be real with God and He will be real with you.

When you go to God be true about your situation God already knows, He is just waiting for you to give it to Him.

(Matthew 6:33)

Seek the Kingdom of God above all else, and live righteously, and he will give you everything you need.

Many people miss out on their blessing because they do the opposite.

They try to get all the world possession and leave God out. God, wants you to come to him first and He will grant you with your desires.

Spend Time with You

After taking time with God, you need to spend time with yourself. Get to know who you are.

You have to get to learn yourself. It's okay to have "me time," with no friends, spouse or children. It's never too late to get to know yourself.

Take time out of your busy schedule and do something you like. Not what your spouse, children or friends like. Do what you enjoy and what makes you happy.

> Treat Yourself To Something Nice.
>
> Take care of you. Others will not take better care of you, than you.
>
> Be *your* biggest fan
>
> Love yourself no matter what
>
> Uplift yourself at all times
>
> Be in control of you. Stop depending so much on others to make you happy
>
> Keep your word
>
> Speak good things about Yourself
>
> You have something amazing to offer this world.
>
> You have a purpose.
>
> Miracles are happening in your life right now!
>
> Believe in You!
>
> Cherish you!

You only have this one life to live, so make the best one EVER!

Keep Your Dreams and Goals to Yourself

Not everyone wants to see you win. People love the thought of you losing and will love to remind you every step of the way.

Have you ever told someone that you were going to do something? And you didn't do it, they were so excited to say how much of a failure you are.

They love to say things like, "I knew you couldn't do it "Those words can cut you.

Unfortunately, the ones that will cut you with those words are usually people that you value. People will try so hard to please others but not enough to satisfy themselves.

Keep all that you want and what want accomplish to yourself. People don't mean well and the last thing you need is for someone to tell you how horrible you are or how much your dreams are impossible.

People put others down because they themselves *don't* think they can accomplish it.

If you get excited, and you want to spread the great news, just remember the thought, they may tell you how much you can't do it.

If you're up for the challenge then great, just remember your goals and dreams need to be **sacred**. If you need someone to tell, *tell it to the Lord*. He will never tell you what you can't do, but what you can do.

Trust yourself

Trust that you can do it. Trust yourself. The problem is not that you have a problem with trusting others, it is trusting yourself.

Trust your gut. Anytime you have that inner feeling to choose A instead of B even though it is going against the grain... Do it! Choose "A."

When that inner voice speaks to you. You know deep down inside what to do.

Some may call it your intuition or the Holy Spirit that lives within you, regardless of what you call it, to trust it. That inner person knows what you need. That inner person is bold, brave and know precisely what you need. Stop second guessing yourself and the choices you make.

Be firm when you make decisions and stick by it no matter the outcome. If this is what you felt in your heart, regardless of what it looks like, go for it.

Trust that voice that you hear. That voice may sound just like your voice, but it is the voice of God speaking to you. Listen to it.

Sometimes it may sound unrealistic, and you may say, I cannot, or that is not realistic. It does not matter take a risk.

This is your life. Choose to live to the best of your ability on your terms, please no one but yourself. It may sound selfish, but it is okay to be selfish if you are taking care of you.

What good are you to people if you are not operating on the best level that you can? Moreover, if you are unhappy, you should look into reassessing your situation and get closer to Christ.

Take care of you and you will be a blessing to others.

Forgive Yourself

Forgive yourself for all your past hurt, disappointments and mistakes you have done to yourself. You are human, and you are not perfect. Stop holding yourself accountable for the hurt that others did to you.

Forgive yourself for all the empty promises that you have told yourself. You have feelings, emotion, and times when you promise yourself things and do come through.

Keep your promises to yourself and see to it that you get those done.

Know Who You Are & Whose You Are

If you know that you don't belong to you, would you treat yourself differently?

Would you walk with your head held high?

Would you walk with purpose?

For some strange reason as people, we will treat others better than we treat ourselves. We will do more for others, than we will do for ourselves. We will even go as far as putting all of our time and energy to learn and manage someone else's dream.

We all are guilty of this. Working for someone 9-5 and giving it our all, but will not take 1 hour out of our busy day to work on our dreams and goals, is simply outrageous.

Do you treat others better than we treat yourself?

Do you care for others more than we care for yourself?

Do you work for others rather than working for yourself?

These are the question you need to think about for a second.

Could it be self-hate? Could it be that you don't love yourself enough? Or maybe you don't believe in yourself enough to manifest your goals and dreams?

During the childhood stages, many children are taught to have respect for others.

> Don't speak to strangers!
>
> Your opinion doesn't matter!
>
> Speak only when you are spoken to!
>
> Don't do that!
>
> Don't go there!
>
> Be back, by this time.
>
> Where are you going?
>
> Why did you do that...? Etc.

These are things as children many people were faced with. For 18 years, someone has been telling you what to do and where to go. How to dress and what to eat? You name it, you have been told everything and as children, and had no voice.

Then adulthood kicks in gear and just like that, you are supposed to become this bold, confident individual that has all the answers. It doesn't work like that.

Many of these rules have stuck with you until now. You are used to people telling you what to do and how to do it. So when it's time for you to think for yourself, it's staggering, nerve recking and scary feeling. I know because I went through it too.

You second guess yourself. You are not sure, and you end up being indecisive. This is another reason why it's so hard to trust yourself and easy to trust other because you used to others telling you what to do.

What if as children you had rules but got the opportunity to think and processes things on your own.

If you had a little bit more independence, do you think it would've change how you operate now?

Well, unfortunately, we can't change the past, but we can create our future.

If in anyway you start to feel that you need someone to guide you, turn to your Heavenly Father. He will never leave you nor forsake you.

Once you are connected to him, you will never feel lonely, unloved or forgotten. Once connected to the source- King Jesus, he will always show you what to do and where to go.

You have to remember that you do not belong to you or just your parents. You belong to a King. You are ROYALTY, and with being a part of the royal family, you have to operate like royalty.

Like a King or Queen. There are places you will not go. Things you will not eat just because you know you are royalty.

Do you believe that you are royalty?

Start changing what you do and how you do it. Start operating like the King and Queen that you are. You are Royalty, and you are a part of the Royal Kingdom. Start treating yourself as such.

No more living below your means and your value. You can do all things through Christ, keep that in mind.

You belong to a higher entity- The Lord Jesus Christ. You do not belong to yourself. You will walk with dignity, purpose, and dominion. God didn't give you a spirit of fear, but of love, power and a sound mind. If you ever reach a place that you feel like you can't move forward, turn to the Lord. He will see you through.

Chapter 7
~*Clutter To Clarity*~

CLUTTER

In all things, you need to have a clear vision. Unfortunately, life is not that well planned out. Many times, you know where you want to go, but have not sense of direction. Not being clear about what you wish to have in life will delay you reaching your destination.

"Out of clutter, find simplicity" -Albert Einstein.

Clutter in all area can hinder you from making decisions for yourself, causing confusion and discomfort. There are many areas in which one can be full of clutter:

- Mental Clutter
- Spiritual Clutter
- Physical Clutter
- Financial Clutter

- Relationship Clutter and more!

Having clutter is not just having a messy house or being a hoarder. Studies show that people that have physical clutter and that is less organize have a tendency to *spend more money*. The reason is that they usually cannot find what they are looking for and have to go and repurchase that item that they already have buried somewhere under something.

Mental Clutter is when you feel like there too much going on in your mind. You may feel overwhelmed and feel like you have no say in what and where you mind is taking you. Mental clutter will make you feel stuck, stress, isolated and frustrated. Mental clutter will also, make you have a full conversation with yourself and talk yourself out of things because of the doubt and insecurities like Rob:

Rob wanted to hang up a painting. He has the painting, nail but no hammer. He decided, he was going to walk over to his neighbor and ask him for a hammer. But at this point, doubt sets in.

Rob thought to himself. "What if my neighbor doesn't want to lend me his hammer? Yesterday, he didn't even speak to me. Maybe he was in a hurry, or perhaps he doesn't like me. But why? I didn't do anything him." He thought to himself.

"How can he refuse to lend me his hammer?" This is unacceptable Rod thought to himself. "I'm going to set him straight."

Rob goes and ring his neighbors doorbell, and before the neighbor could say anything, Rob screams: "YOU CAN KEEP YOUR DAMN HAMMER, YOU BASTARD!!"

Spiritual Clutter can sabotage your spiritual life and your relationship with God. Spiritual Clutter is a feeling of fear, sorrow, guilt resentment or jealousy. Leaving no space for God because you are filled with all the negative trash that has taken up residence in our minds and spirit.

Physical Clutter represents what is going on in our minds. Seeing the physical clutter over and over generates more mental clutter, stress, and confusion in our mind. It also causes major distractions. Physical clutter is a representation of our home, car, office and other area that accumulate mess. Messiness is a form of physical clutter.

Financial Clutter is expensive. Not being in the loop of what is going on in your finances can cause financial clutter. Having multiple bank accounts, credit cards, debts or assets. Many people have so many credit cards and cannot manage it to the point they get frustrated and do nothing with them. They don't pay anything on them, and this is what usually cause credit issues.

Sometime people forget who they owe and how much they owe. Mismanagement of one's finances causes financial clutter.

Relationship Clutter is energy that is stagnant and prevents you from living the life you desire and deserve. In your relationship, clutter stems from you bringing *baggage, old habits* and *feelings* into the new relationship. A new person does not deserve to be treated like the previous person from your past.

The ancient Chinese proverb, *"A cluttered space equals a cluttered mind."*

Now that we are clear on what clutter consists of, the real question is how to declutter these areas.

Declutter

Clean up your mind, body, and spirit. Everything starts in your mind. That is the first area that you will have to clean up to see the cleanliness manifest in other areas.

> *Declutter your Mind*
>
> *Declutter your Spirit*
>
> *Declutter your Space*

Declutter your Finances

Declutter your Relationship

Declutter your Mind is prioritizing what thoughts are worth thinking, and the other thoughts cancel them. What helps with decluttering your mind is writing & journaling. Having an area to get all your thoughts on paper. This is free up space in your mind to all new and healthy thoughts.

During the morning and throughout your day when you start to get those overwhelming thoughts, write it down on paper immediately you will begin to feel better.

Your mind is a battlefield. So many thoughts in so little time. You have to take time out and allow those thoughts to develop through your mind like clouds that will cause a major thunderstorm. If you write it down, this will help with running those thoughts out of you leisurely to recognize the potential that you want to be the center.

After getting those thoughts out of your way, then get a journal and write about all the essential events you want to think about and what you want to manifest. Look at that paper three times a day and start meditating on what's on the paper. This will help to shift your thinking and help you control those thoughts floating through your mind.

Declutter your spirit is to make God the center. Spend time with God. Spend time in prayer and meditation. This will allow you to release all of those negative feelings and thoughts you may have.

When you spend time with God, he will take away the negative and fill you up with positive loving, self-worth and confidence. There will be no room for negativity. Add God to your morning routine, and this will set the pace for the rest of your day.

Prayer changes things. Keep God in the midst of everything that you are doing. Your spirit is very delicate. Be careful of what you listen to, watch on television and what you spend most of your time doing.

Your spirit needs to stay connected with Lord Jesus Christ. Spend time with him by praying and if this is new to you, put yourself on a schedule when to pray. Also, pray for as long as you need to. Don't pray just one sentence, talk to God let him know what's going on, what your desire are and where you want to be. Also, pray for people you are around.

God already knows, he wants you to bring it to him. In the beginning, it may feel a little weird if you haven't prayed before, but as you continue, then you will see and feel the difference when you pray.

Declutter your space, remember that your space is a reflection of your mind. If your space is a mess then start to put yourself on a schedule. Yes, you are only one person and sometimes the clutter has gotten so bad that you may not know where or even how to begin. Start with areas that people will see first if they were to come to your home. Start with scheduling a to-do list in the prioritized order that matters the most. Your schedule should look something like this:

Monday 7 pm, clean the kitchen and go into details:

Wash the dishes, clean the stove, microwave and refrigerator... etc.

Tuesday 7 pm, clean the bathroom... etc.

Prioritizing and scheduling will help get you to where you want to be quicker than you trying to do it. Your space is something that you look at every day. Your home is your **Castle**, you have to take care of it. Again: Cleanliness is next to Godliness.

Your castle is a representation of who you are. Yes, that means if you have dishes in your sink and dirty clothing that says you have clutter in your mind. Take time out of your busy schedule and clean up your space.

Clean up your space.

It will make you feel better which will help eliminate the clutter physically and mentally. Don't wait until your home is a complete disaster before you start cleaning again, but do it every day a little at a time. That will help you keep it clean. As you use something put it right back when you are done. That will help keep you on track with keeping your castle clean.

If you can afford it and you will like to hire someone, then by all means, get someone in there to do the spring cleaning no matter what time of the year it is.

Declutter your finances will allow you to manage and know exactly what's going on in your finances. Your finances cannot manage itself. You have to be in the loop with what is going on with your finances. You should not check your bank account and guess the amount that is in there. You should already know.

It is your finances, you have to take responsibility. You need to know every transaction that is taking place.

One of the things that help me to declutter my finances is having a calendar and writing all my monthly bills down and adding them to the calendar each month. I started off with a physical calendar and later move it to a digital calendar. Digital is easier because you can have access to it at all the time.

That helped me stay in the loop with my finances. My finances was all over the place. Transactions were happening and I had no clue. I would get up one morning with a lot of money and the next morning with a negative balance and could not understand what was going on.

I had to take a stand and discipline my self. I discipline my spending habits and started to get obsessed with my finances and my credit. I started watching videos and reading books on how to manage my finances.

Then while being disciplined, I realized I had very bad spending habits. Guess what? I hated bringing lunch to work. When I add up how much I spent at work for the month, it was over $250, and I thought to myself, that could've been added to my savings that month. I had to make a change. Just buying coffee, a full breakfast and lunch each day was breaking me. I said! "Wait just a minute!"

That was a lot of money I spent at work. Not to mention my husband and children eating out for dinner on some nights. It was a disaster.

I created some steps that help me and my family declutter our finances, and it will also help you.

- Organize the inward flow of your money
- Minimize your bank accounts
- Gather all of your credit cards
- Close all of you credit cards you are not using
- Get a copy off your credit report
- Set up automatic payment for bills
- Minimize your spending
- Save a little at a time
- Bring your lunch to work

These steps are elementary but very effective. These steps allowed to manage my finances and help others do the same. A little goes a long way.

Management

In life, greatness happens when you manage a particular thing. Whatever you manage will succeed, whatever you don't manage will fail.

Time management, you know is super important, but what about those other areas that people don't talk about as much. You need to learn to manage all areas of your life, if you want it to succeed.

For example:

In a marriage, if both parties do not spend time with one another and make and effort to communicate, will quickly end a marriage. No communication and quality time spent is a form of mismanagement in a relationship because it can make or break a marriage. Putting forth no-effort can also be a form of mismanagement of a marriage and result in a divorce.

If a mom doesn't take the time out of her busy schedule to assist her age-old elementary child with his or her homework is a form of mismanagement. What about not spending time looking through her child test results and report cards, to see the areas the child needs help, and the child begins to fail. This is also considered mismanagement on the mom, for not assisting the child in the needed area. Scheduling is a priority! Mismanagement or Management, it's either one or the other.

Mis-management is not being in the loop of what going on. Not taking the time and making sure all is well, not making sure that everything is ran smoothly and not communicating with the other party as to what to expect. You may not think that is mismanagement, but that's what it is.

Management is making sure everything is moving according to plan, running the way you expected it to be and to make sure that you have communicated correctly to the correct parties as to what is expected.

In any area, you want to succeed or be great be sure that you are managing that area correctly, whether it's a relationship, children, marriage, friendship or your home, vehicle, etc.

If you want a better result, start to manage those problem area or areas, and watch the results begin to shift

Power of Saying NO!

Many people think saying No is being mean or not being Christ-like. Some people believe that if they say "No" to an individual, they are not living according to the word of God. You may agree with this theory, but it is also impossible to say "YES" to everything or every situation that occur in your life.

You must say NO! If it's something that is harming you spiritually, emotionally, mentally or physically you must say "No!" Stop allowing others to tell you what you must do and how to do it and start trusting that inner voice.

I know a lot of people that want to give everything to others, but won't do the same for themselves. If you are always giving and they are regularly taking, then who is giving to you?

I know some may say- God will give it and yes to an extent. If someone is blatantly taking advantage of you and you're allowing them to do it, that this is a problem. You must get to a place that you love yourself so much, that you won't let that happen to you repeatedly.

I sadly believe that many people don't care if they are using others because people are very selfish. You are better than that. People will respect you if you respect yourself.

Using others is a very selfish act, and unfortunately, a lot of people do it without a care in the world of the other person's feelings. Don't allow others to use you. Become selfish enough to love yourself, and care for yourself that you won't let others use you.

Knowing What You Want

Be very clear about what you want. When you go to God, go to him with clarity. Life is too short not to know what you want out of it. Make it your duty to figure out what you want in all areas of your life.

Make a list of what you want. Here are some questions you need to ask yourself and on a separate piece of paper answer them:

> What type of relationship do you want?

What type of spouse are you looking for?

Is he or she family oriented, smart, loving and kind?

Do you want a business?

What type of business do you want?

How much do you want to make in your business?

Do you want $100 or $10,000 more a month?

Do you want a 6 figure, 7 figure or just an extra $50,000 a year?

Do you want employees?

Do you want an office?

Do you want children?

Do you want more children, if you already have?

Do want a house?

What type of house do you want?

How many bedrooms and bathrooms do you want?

Where do you want to live?

Have you ever been to that neighborhood before?

How much does it cost?

How much do you need to make to own that home?

What is your dream car?

What's the make and model?

How much does it cost?

What color is it?

Will your immediate family fit in the car?

After answering these questions.

Create the life you want first in your mind.

Write it down. Try to be as detailed as possible. Don't leave any gray areas.

Review your list daily 3x a day.

Focus on it throughout the day

Habits

Habits can make you or break you. Habits are settled, regular tendency or practices. Some habits that are hard to give up.

What are your habits? Are they good or bad?

Shopping is one habit I know can be a nightmare for some that are trying to increase their savings. Not being able to control that shopping habit can you feel horrible because the money spent could have gone into their savings account.

Habits, whether it is good or bad, can sometimes be hard to break. Studies show to break any habit it will take a minimum of **21 days**.

My personal opinion, I think it depends on what the habit is determines the length it will take to break it. Many will say that smoking is a bad habit.

I knew individuals that have smoked for over 36 years. Do you think it will take 21 days to break that habit? No, especially if they don't believe they can do it.

For example: My brother had a bad habit of smoking, however: he just woke up one day and he said "I quit"! And just like that, he quit. Now that sounds like outstanding will power.

Will power and believing that you can is root of getting over bad habits.

If you have a habit, then change your patterns. Remember that your mind is more powerful than you think it is. You will need to replace that bad habit with a good one. I know, I know it sounds easier than it really is.

Bad habits can prevent you from accomplishing your goals and interrupt your life. Stress, anxiety, and boredom cause lousy habits.

It's only hard if you believe it's hard.

Here is a list of some good practices you can use to replace those bad habits:

> Affirmations
> Pray
> Laugh
> Write down positive things about yourself
> Write down your thoughts
> Listen and watch motivational videos
> Read
> Mediate
> Sleep- get 8 hours of sleep
> Exercise to increase your energy
> Hobby
> Treat yourself
> Surround yourself with positive people
> Chew gym
> Go outside and enjoy the sun

Focus on the positive things in life
Think positive
Connect with people that are where you want to be
Eat Healthier foods
Save money
Spend less
Set goals with a deadline
Make time for yourself

Along with your willpower, believing technique and visualizing yourself succeeding. You will create your new identity. Your habits can define you. Change your bad habits to good habits and make it count.

CHAPTER 8
~VISION~

WRITE THE VISION

Your vision belongs to you. Only *you* know what you want out of life. Every day of your life, your goal you should be discovering *how can you make this vision that I you have become your reality.*

Do you have a vision? What is your vision?

Even if it takes 30 years to accomplish your vision it's never too late. Many have tried to accomplish their dreams and goals with only one attempt. You have to keep pushing. The obstacle will come and that is a part of life.

You have to keep pushing and pushing through the pain. Some nights you may get frustrated, you may cry, you may even want to give up. But, YOU CANNOT QUIT! No matter how tough it gets, you have to keep pushing.

In 2013, a woman name Diana Nyad shows a perfect example of not giving up no matter how many failed attempts.

At the age of 64, Diana finally completes her lifetime vision, goal and dream. Her vision was completing a 100 mile swim from Cuba to Florida. Diana Nyad made 5 attempts before completing this dream of hers, swimming along with sharks and jellyfish in the infested murky waters.

At the age of 29 was her first attempt at completing this journey in 1978. At that time the seas were rough and fought. She was bruised and battered halfway towards her goal.

She tried twice in 2011, but had an asthma attack and was severely stung by jellyfish.

Her third attempt she made it halfway there and the weather was terrible. There was a lightning storm which super dangerous, and again she was severely stung by jellyfish.

At this point, any regular person would have given up and threw in the towel, but Dania did not. She kept pushing forward. Just for the record, Diana was a well-trained swimmer that won many swimming marathons and was the first woman to swim around the Island of Manhattan.

She dreamt about swimming in the ocean to Florida since the age of 8 and had of sense of urgency.

Diana kept pushing. On her fifth attempt at the age of 64, without the aid of a shark cage, she was stressed out and did not think that this would've been her final attempt. She gave it her all.

She did it! She didn't allow that voice in her head to tell her she was too old or she was not physically capable to do it. She didn't allow all the naysayers to keep her down. She didn't give up on her dreams.

You are never too old to give up on your dreams. Keep pushing until you get it done. You want to leave this earth as a person remembered as that person who faced their obstacles and conquered them.

Know your vision, write out your vision and achieve your vision.

Write the vision and make it plain on paper.

>*You can do it!*

>*You can achieve it!*

>*Stay the course!*

>*You are not too old!*

>*You are not too young!*

>*You can do all things through Christ!*

>*I believe in you and You need to believe in yourself!*

Waiting Until the Time Is Right

"Do not wait: the time will never be 'just right'. Start where you stand, and work whatever tools you may have at your command and better tools will be found as you go along."   - Napoleon Hill-

"Just do it," like Nike says. The perfect time to get started does NOT exist. You will be waiting for a lifetime if you are waiting for the perfect time.

>*I can't do it!*

>*I'm too tired!*

>*Now is not the right time!*

>*Maybe tomorrow!*

>*I can't focus right now!*

>*I have too much to do!*

Nobody will help me!

I'm not smart enough!

I just don't know how to do it!

I waiting for someone to help me!

One day I will do it!

I don't have the money!

I don't have the resources!

I don't have the...

Now, that we got that out of the way, **I'm going to grab a garbage can and you can put every excuse in it**. Every *I can't, I don't, Not and I'm not....* Right in the garbage and start focusing on what you can do. This is a cycle that many people are caught in and it's so hard for them to break free from it. People are so afraid to just do! Just stand up and be strong and do something meaningful.

If it feels right, then it is right.

Challenge yourself to be great. Step out of your comfort zone and do something that you actually care about. Stop rationalizing why you can't and start thinking of reasons why YOU CAN.

People will go their whole lives not stepping out and trying something that is meaningful to them. So many people live through those people that do step out of their comfort zone and do something great. **We all have the same amount of hours, minutes and days of the week to try something new and be great.**

Tell me what you are capable of!

When will you have time?

What resources you do have?

Nothing or nobody will stop you!

You will get started now no matter what.

You have to get out of the habit of focusing on what you cannot do and start to focus on what you can do. It is so easy to come up with excuses and every reason in the world you can't get started.

What is Your Why?

What is the reason why you will get started? The reason why you have to do it. The reason why you cannot give up. The reason why everything inside of you will not let you quit. That reason can be your husband, children, mom, and family because others said you cannot or just for you. You are worth it. Your why is important enough, that's why you cannot quite!

The time will never be right. You will always have something or someone trying to stop you from moving forward. You have to keep pushing. As you push, things and the right people will start being attracted to you. They will want to work with you and help you make your dream a reality. You have to know that you have the ability to get the job done no matter what it looks like.

Every moment that you can work on your dreams, do it.

Invest In You

It's funny how people will put so much energy and effort to build someone else's dreams and not build their own. You have to start investing in yourselves every chance you get.

"You will never go broke from investing in yourself" - Anonymous-

Stepping out of that bubble and allowing yourselves to invest in *you* will be worth it. The first step in investing in yourself is getting started. If you decide to go back to school, *get started!* If you decide to start that business, *get started!* If you decide to do anything, *get started!*

The first hurdle is the hardest but once you get started, you will see how things will just fall into place.

You have everything you need. Yes, you may have to seek a little assistance if it is an area you are unfamiliar with. You have to take time to invest in self-development. Depending on others will never get you where you want to be. However, if you invest in yourself you will be where you want to be.

"It is better to live your own destiny imperfectly than to live an imitation of somebody else's life with perfection." -Anonymous-

You have something amazing to offer this world. You can do it! Just believe in yourself and you will get it done!

Vision Board

After writing the vision, the next step is to see your vision. Creating a vision board will allow you to visualize your written dreams. According to the law of attraction, visualization is extremely powerful with manifesting your dreams.

A vision board is a collection of images, photos, quotes in different area like: finances, career, personal growth, home, relationship education, and health, spiritual and social life. Places that you will like to travel. It's just a glimpse of where and what you will like to be manifested in your life.

"Thoughts become things" - Law of attraction

The goal is to go there in your mind first and then it will manifest in your reality.

A vision board will also help you stay focus on where you want to be. When life happens it can sometimes be devastating. Sometimes it can hit you so hard you forget where you want to be. The vision board is a reminder for those days that you feel like giving up and when you feel like you cannot do it.

The vision board will keep all of your dreams and goals in a visualized matter in one location. The vision board will allow you to see it and it will be some much easier to believe it.

You will gain clarity and maximize your visual practice. Vision boards are also known as dream boards, goal & inspiration boards. The images on your vision board will help strengthen and stimulate your emotions and subconscious mind.

The ultimate goal is to look at your vision board daily with the visuals you placed on a poster board or a digital poster with images, the collage of words that represents your dreams and goals.

A good suggestion is to take a picture of the board and look at it when you are away from it. The goal is to dwell on the board as much as possible. This will shift your feeling and will make you feel subconsciously that you are where you want to be while you are dwelling on your vision board.

Honesty Is Still the Best Policy

Be honest with yourself and your situation. Take some time out of your busy schedule and reflect on your day. Do not try to be anyone else but yourself. You are the only one that can make a change in your life.

If you are honest with yourself then it will be easier to identify the areas you will like a change.

For example: Stop pretending like you have it all together and you don't. If you are a mom and your desire is to have a clean home but, because of your children, you are unable to keep your home clean. Stop going out and telling others how you have it all together when in actuality you are a mess. You have to get to a place of realization of being real with you.

The first step to an addiction is realizing and admitting that there is a problem. Many times we have the tendency to not want to admit that we have an issue and just want miracles to happen in our lives.

You have to be real with your situation. If you are on the verge of being broke, but want a financial breakthrough and your habits are not changing your negative habits, then you're not being real > with yourself. Remember the definition of insanity-Wanting to change your outcome but doing the same actions looking for a better result.

"God helps those that help themselves" - Anonymous

Many may agree and some may disagree with this statement but God will truly help all. God will help you in all areas of your life, however, at the same time, "Faith without works is dead." Putting in the work and being real with yourself and God, he will truly help you get out of the situation that you are in and put you where you want to be.

Get to know who you are, what you like and where you want to be in life. Give it to God and believe that a change will come, but while you are waiting to continue to work on yourself. Continue to make room for God in your everyday decisions, but don't leave God out of any of your plans.

Learn to trust God because God wants the best for you. He wants you to live an abundant life. He wants you to be great. God also wants you to have an amazing and rich life. He does not want you to be poor or live a life filled with hurt and depression. He has to be the source of your life. God has to be your lifeline. Spend time with him, give it all to him and he will work it out.

Keep It 100

Keep it real. No more faking it. Now in some areas, you can fake it till you make it, it will help elevate you. Don't fake it till you make it, if it's going to harm you or put you into deeper debt.

Be real with you and be real with God. God already knows he is just waiting for you to give it to him. Remember God does not lie. So why do we? Do not lie to God! If you made a promise to God keep it. If you made a promise to yourself keep that also.

When you make a promise keep it. Let your Yes be Yes, and your No be No.

BELIEVE IN YOURSELF · 100

Chapter 9
~Keep Winning~

WINNERS KEEP WINNING

Winners are no different from losers. The only difference is that winners did not give up. We all have failed at something in life or had wished that we could have kept going. Keep pushing and never giving up no matter what! This is what sets apart winners from losers. People think that winners just woke up and life was handed to them, or they feel like winners have never failed before.

Every winner I know have said that they have failed from time to time. Some winner will tell you that they made up in their minds that no matter what, how many times they failed, they never gave up and will not give up.

For some, failure is a reflection of not being good enough. To others, failure is a determination to be great and they will succeed no matter what.

If you have tried something and have failed and try again and failed again that's, okay. **You are just one step closer to winning.** Failures often leads to success.

A great man that many know of is the famous Michael Jordan. He was cut from his high school basketball team in his sophomore year. He took that as a determination to never give up and to keep pushing. His failure motivated him to work hard.

He has missed 9,000 shots in his career and has lost close to 300 games. But he never gave up. He kept his eyes on the prize and won many games and received several awards for his accomplishments.

Though many had told him he could not do it, and he will never make it. He did not quit. When others were out playing, he stayed focused. He continued to work on his craft. He worked on it so much he became an expert.

Being a winner is not easy. I know you may want to give up and throw in the towel, but don't. You may even cry because you want to succeed so bad and you will succeed if you stay focus and keep pushing.

Remember your success is not just about you. People are depending on you. Your spouse, mom, dad, your children, family members, church members, youth group and many more individuals are depending on you to succeed.

You have to do it. You have no choice. Others are depending on you.

You cannot quit!

You cannot give up!

You can make it!

Stay the course!

Stay focus!

You got this!

Operate in Excellence

In everything give God your best! Give others your best and even your employer, even if they don't deserve it. Don't operate below your standards for others. Do not operate below your level of excellence.

You may think people are not watching you, but unfortunately, they are. Everyone is watching including God, Himself. For some strange reason, we operate better when we know others are watching.

In all things do your best.

(*Galatian 6:9*) Let us not become weary in doing good, for at the proper time we will reap a harvest if we do not give up.

We need to keep doing our best no matter what. We will reap the reward that we do from the Lord. It will not come from the employer or a friend telling us to keep up the good work, but it will come from the Lord.

Times will get tough and there are times when you may want to give up, but fight the good fight.

(**Psalm 75:6-7**) For promotion cometh neither from the east or the west, nor from the south. But God is the judge: He putteth down one, and setteth up another

If no one else sees your hard work, God does and He will promote you. Promotion comes from God. We may think it comes from your manager or supervisor, but the Lord is the one that will allow your promotion to come to past.

"Where much is giving, much is required" - (*Luke 12:48*)

You have to be honest and hardworking over the little things, then God will promote you to bigger and better things.

Passion Is Power

"Doing what you love you will never work a day in your life"
~Anonymous

> *What are you passionate about?*
>
> *What is something you cannot stop thinking about?*
>
> *What makes you happy?*
>
> *What do you do with no effort but do it so well?*
>
> *What do you love doing?*

After answering these questions, you will be closer to what you are passionate about. A plethora of people feel stuck and feel like there is no way out. Many are working dead-end jobs or feel like, this is it to life. I'm here to let you know, there is more to life. So much more!

It is still so much you can accomplish. Ignite the fire within you. Continue to have faith and give it to God and He will work it out.

Your past does not dictate your future. Just because in your past you have done things that were not pleasing to God, others or yourself doesn't mean it can't get better. It can always get better, but you have to believe that it can.

Your future awaits you. All good things are waiting for you in your future. Don't give up! Don't quit! You can have the life you desire, the career and salary you desire, including all the other great things you want out of this life. God wants you to have an abundant life. God has done away with your past. He has put your past in the sea of forgetfulness.

If your past years were amazing, but now the life you are living at the moment is not what you desire, you still have an opportunity to make a change. As long as you have breath in your body, you have another chance at this thing we call life.

I know it may be rough, especially if you are surrounded by negative people that I like to call dream killers. Change your circle of friends, relatives, or business partners and start operating in your purpose with passion. You can have it all. I believe that you can and you will.

Be passionate about your desires in life. Don't go through life feeling sorry for yourself or feeling down. Elevate your spirit. Go back to those things that made you smile or laugh. That thing that brought energy back into your life.

Start spending time with people that desire to be in your presence. You only have this one life to live with this one temple God loan you. So while you are here on earth make it count. Get excited about life again! Get excited about God again or even get excited about your spouse! Remember you could have been on the other side of life, but instead, you are above the ground so be grateful.

Forgive those that hurt you and have a clean slate. Tomorrow is a new day. Ask God to renew your mind as the day begin for you to allow positive energy to flow through your life.

Once you allow yourself to operate in your passion, you begin to love yourself again. Your conversations will change, your feelings will change. You will feel unstoppable.

Once you are aligned with God you will be so powerful that nothing or nobody will be able to stop you. Even when those tough days come, it will just roll off. You will know exactly how to deal with it.

When you are operating in your purpose you will know how to deal with those negative people and you will start to easily avoid listening to those negative remarks about yourself or about others.

Your heart will feel lighter. You will feel strong in all the right areas of your life.

Confident Journal

Get a journal. No, not a diary, but a journal. In this journal, you want to put all good things about yourself. Think of it as a gratitude journal. You may already have a journal, which is great, but in this journal, there are some specific key things you will need to add.

Writing is a way of expressing yourself. Especially, if you do not have an outlet. Journaling can be that outlet.

Writing saved my life. I wrote not only about my day and about all the things I hated, but I shifted my writing and started writing where I wanted to be. I started to add photos and other great things to get me excited about being me. I know for a fact that your experience will supersede mine.

In this confident journal, here are some key things that you may add

Photo of you smiling

Affirmations

Things that you like about yourself

Things that you want to accomplish

What your passion?

What is your purpose in life?

Places you will like to visit

Things you enjoy doing

People that adore you

Your dreams and goals

Financial goals

Career goals

Family goals

Spiritual goals

Photos to capture the visual

Where do you see yourself in the next 5 years?

Long-term goals with a deadline of when it will be accomplished

Short-term goals with a deadline of when it will be accomplished

Add any other great things about yourself. This journal will help to remind you of who you are and where you will like to be.

Life has a way of beating us down or reminding us how great we are not. So, in this journal, it will help you to keep all of those good thoughts, feelings, and desires that you have one area It will
help keep your focus on the great you and not the horrible or past you.

People are always quick to remind us of who we were and about our past, but all we have to say is "BUT GOD". God has changed you and delivered you from your old ways.

I cannot wait to see all the great things you will accomplish. **I Believe In YOU!**

My Journey to Believing in Myself

As a child, I never thought I fit into any crowd. I was not like anyone else and I knew it. I tried hanging out with different crowds but never felt like a perfect fit.

I moved around a lot as a child. I lived in different states and even moved out of the United States. Florida became my home during middle school.

We lived in many apartments and even with my mom friends. I remember going to at least five different elementary schools.

I had a unique accent at this point trying to adapt to my surroundings. That was the perfect tool for kids to make fun of me.

By the time we settled, I started Middle School and by that time, my parents were separated. I got into so many fights. Every other day my mom was at my school because some girl was trying to fight me.

I did not have a relationship with God and we did not go to church. When Sundays came around, we would play soft music. I guess that was our way of honoring God.

I knew of God but did not know God.

That is a big difference.

In Middle School and High School, I never felt good enough or pretty enough. Not to mention I grew up in a broken home.

My Dad was not around during my teenage years due to his line of work. That was the time I felt I needed him the most. Most girls need their fathers, especially around that time. I had no one to tell me I was beautiful and I could do anything I put my mind to. For the record my mom did tell me those things, however, every girl needs to hear that from their father.

What do girls normally do when they do not have their father there every day? They turn to boys.

When I became a teenager, my mom was literally all I had. My father at the time lived in Jamaica so during that time it was just a phone call kind of relationship or occasional visits here and there.

I met this boy and all I can say he was NOT good for me. What I thought was love quickly turned into verbal abuse and later into physical abuse.

I was in a very unhealthy relationship. I remained with this guy for quite some time. I continue to take the abuse because I thought that was love.

I had no clue what love looked like from a man. During high school, this guy remained my boyfriend. I took this abuse for a long time and never told anyone. Being that I was so determined to be someone great in life. I join the Majorette team at my school. Joined the SGA club to try to fill a void that I was missing.

I started working while still in school and thought my life was not that bad. Had a job at the Mall and still was on the majorette team and thought life was getting better. After graduating high school I wanted to move back to New York and pursue my Fashion career and then I found out I was pregnant.

I was so hurt. I was so lost and I was so heartbroken.

I know I was in no position to be a mother. I had just graduated high school and was about to start college. I could not believe this was my life. I did not know how to cook and barely knew how to clean. I talked so bad about teenage moms and now I was one. My life flashed before my eyes. I was so afraid to tell anyone. I told my boyfriend and he was happy. I just cried and cried and cried.

I finally build up enough courage to tell my mom. Before I said anything to her, she told me, I was pregnant. I do not know if it was an Island thing, but I always heard that moms always know. I was so afraid. I thought she was going to scream at me or kick me out the house. I just did not know what was going to happen.

My mom told me she got me, and I will be okay. I was so shocked by her response. I couldn't believe it. I told my mom as long as she supports me, I know I could do it.

Now it was time for the family to know. I did not want to tell them.

When the family found out, they talked so bad about me. They made me feel like nothing and my mom always had my back no matter what.

They told me I will never be anything in life and I am just another statistic.

While being pregnant I continued to take the abuse from my boyfriend, who was soon to be the father of my child.

In my heart, I knew this was not good and I did not want to raise my child in this.

Months later I gave birth to my beautiful bundle of joy. I was so in love with this little person. I had this unexplainable unconditional love for my new baby girl.

After a couple of months of getting the hang of motherhood, my mom then told me that she was moving to Jamaica, and she will help me for a year and then she was leaving the States. All I had was my mom. She was my everything.

My mom always was there for me, so for her to leave I didn't know how I was going to do it by myself. I was just getting the hang of this motherhood thing.

I thought once I had my baby my relationship would've gotten better, but it only got worse.

My daughter turned one and that was my cut off for my mom to move.

It was me and my little princess. Months went by and I started to get the hang of being on my own. I got my place started college and finally felt like an adult. Not long after, I started not feeling well. As a matter of fact, few weeks later, I found out I was pregnant again.

Once again, I'm at this place of being broken, hurt and feeling like a true disappointment. I knew the family was going to have a field day talking about me all over again. Just when I thought it was over my life was getting worse by the minute.

Teen mom with no money, no support from the dad, and I was pregnant again. This could not be my life. I did not know what to do. I was still a child with a child and pregnant with another one. I felt so lost.

I felt so defeated. I officially felt like a statistic. I thought to myself, I will never be anything in life just a "baby momma." I wanted more for my life. I did not want it to be like this. I felt so defeated and felt like I was nothing and will never be anything.

At this time my kids' father could not keep a job would not help me and I had to do it all by myself.

I started going to church and I didn't know much about the Lord, but I went and just listened. My cousin invited me and I just loved how I felt being in church. I learned so much about the Lord. Going to church made everything feel okay.

I started attending church every Sunday and decided that I wanted to get baptized.

Unfortunately, I continued seeing this guy. I continued taking the abuse from him. I felt trapped. I felt like I didn't have a way out.

But I was determined to get out of this toxic relationship. I told God, if he gets me out of this I will serve him all my days.

Time passed and I joined the church. I started to bring my kids every Sunday and felt so full in my spirit. I learned how God loved me and how he purified me. I started to learn that God has the final say over my life, not man. I felt so renewed.

I told myself I wanted more and I believe after hearing the word of God, that I can have all that my heart desires.

So one day I told myself, no more. I'm not taking this anymore. **Enough is enough**!

I made up my mind and I was not taking it anymore. On that day things got so violent. He started arguing with me and things got ugly. It was the worst day of my life, but at the same time a new beginning.

After that day, I never looked back. With all that I went through, I thank God for my children. God gave me two amazing children out of that crazy mess of a relationship. I continued to go to church and learn about that Loved of God.

I also learned how important it was for me to think highly of myself. I know in my heart that Jesus loved me unconditionally. I felt like I got my life back. This love I felt, I have never felt it before.

No more hurt, pain or disappointment. I started to tell others about how good God is. My mom and my sister got saved. I felt so full in my heart. I didn't care about what people thought of me anymore. I knew Jesus loved me and my children. I knew in my heart that we were going to be okay. The Lord gave me confidence that I never had. I felt so beautiful and started to love myself and believed in myself.

I wanted the best for myself and my family. No one never taught me that my mindset had everything to do with what I attracted. Once I learn the power of my thoughts my life change for the better and every day I woke with the mindset that I can accomplish anything if I only believed.

God blessed me with an amazing, intelligent, handsome, loving, God fearing husband that **loves me for me** and my children. God also blessed us with two more amazing children. My life is filled with so much joy and happiness.

I'm now a wife, mother of 4, Certified Life Coach, Educator, Mentor and Entrepreneur. I live a lifestyle of empowering individuals to build their confidence, believe in themselves and become unstoppable.

My goal is to promote self-love, confidence building, positive thinking, self-motivation and uplifting self-esteems.

Don't let anyone tell you can't live the life you desire. If you want better, change your mindset and change your situation. You no longer have to feel stuck. God did it for me and He can do it for you. Believe that your situation can change and it will.

Believe that you can and you will!

I AM

Take a moment and create your **AFFIRMATIONS** and what you **BELIEVE** for your life.

I BELIEVE in MYSELF
I BELIEVE _____
I BELIEVE _____
I BELIEVE _____
I BELIEVE _____
I BELIEVE _____
I BELIEVE _____
I BELIEVE _____
I BELIEVE _____
I BELIEVE _____

I AM the head and not the tail
I AM _____
I AM _____
I AM _____
I AM _____
I AM _____
I AM _____
I AM _____
I AM _____
I AM _____

I CAN do ALL things through Christ who strengthen me
I CAN _____
I CAN _____
I CAN _____
I CAN _____
I CAN _____
I CAN _____
I CAN _____
I CAN _____
I CAN _____

www.ingramcontent.com/pod-product-compliance
Lightning Source LLC
Chambersburg PA
CBHW070952080526
44587CB00015B/2276